FAITH
WALKING
through
PROBLEMS

FAITH
WALKING
through
PROBLEMS

ELMER L. TOWNS

DESTINY IMAGE® PUBLISHERS, INC.
P.O. Box 310, Shippensburg, PA 17257-0310
"Promoting Inspired Lives."

This book and all other Destiny Image and Destiny Image Fiction books are available at Christian bookstores and distributors worldwide.

For more information on foreign distributors, call 717-532-3040.

Reach us on the Internet: www.destinyimage.com.

ISBN 13 TP: 978-0-7684-7176-2

ISBN 13 eBook: 978-0-7684-7177-9

For Worldwide Distribution.

1 2 3 4 5 6 7 8 / 27 26 25 24 23

CONTENTS

PART THREE

PART FOUR

Introduction

FAITH-WALKING THROUGH PROBLEMS

*We can rejoice, too, when we run into
problems and trials, for we know they
help us to develop strong faith.*

Romans 5:3, ELT

GOD created a perfect world, with a perfect environment, and then put perfect people there to live a perfect life. Adam and Eve were created perfect. "So God created man in his own image, in the image of God created he him; male and female created he them" (Genesis 1:27). Since God is the blueprint and/or model for the first couple, how else could they be created?

God gave them one commandment with both a positive and negative implication: "You may freely eat the fruit of every tree in the garden—except the tree of the knowledge of good and evil. If you eat its fruit, you are sure to die" (Genesis 2:16-17, NLT).

The man and woman did not have a sinful nature, nor were they inclined to disobey God. Sin—with its problems and suffering—came from outside the man and woman. "The serpent was the shrewdest of all the wild animals the Lord God had made. One day he asked the woman, 'Did God really say you must not eat the fruit from any of the trees in the garden?'" (Genesis 3:1, NLT). The serpent—satan—placed doubt in the woman's mind by questioning the command that God had given them. And from that doubt came the woman's conversation with the serpent/satan. She said, "God said, 'You must not eat it or even touch it; if you do, you will die'" (Genesis 3:3, ESV).

"You won't die," the serpent lied to Eve (Genesis 3:4). As a result she ate the fruit, then gave some to her husband who was with her. He disobeyed God and ate.

"At that moment their eyes were opened, and they suddenly felt shame at their nakedness" (Genesis 3:7). Sin or disobedience affects not only our spiritual perceptions to see God, but it also makes the temptations of the world real to us. One of the first things the couple did was to clothe themselves because they were naked.

Sin had various consequences on the couple. To the woman God said, "I will sharpen the pain of your pregnancy, and in pain you will give birth" (Genesis 3:16, NLT).

To the man God said, "The ground is cursed because of you. All your life you will struggle to scratch a living from it. It will grow thorns and thistles for you, though you will eat of its grains. By the sweat of your brow will you have food to eat until you return to the ground from which you were made. For you were made from dust, and to dust you will return" (Genesis 3:17-19, NLT).

When God originally told Adam and Eve, "You will surely die" (Genesis 3:3), there was a twofold consequence to the word "die." First, Adam died immediately, which is *spiritual death*. Adam was separated from God and the only way he could live with God for all eternity was to have his sins forgiven and to be given entrance into the presence of God. This was done through the *Second Adam*, i.e., the Lord Jesus Christ who died for the sins of Adam and Eve, plus the sins of the entire world.

Then Adam died a second way: he died physically. Not immediately, but he began to die, and the Bible says, "Adam lived 930 years, and then he died" (Genesis 5:5). From this story we find the introduction of sin, pain, suffering, and agony. Not only in this present life is there temporary pain and suffering, but there will be eternal pain and suffering in hell for those who do not believe in Jesus Christ for salvation.

PART ONE

FAITH
WALKING
through
PROBLEMS

Chapter 1

APPROACHING PROBLEMS IN YOUR LIFE

WHEN you think about pain and suffering, ask yourself three questions: "Why me?" "Why now?" "Why this?"

Even as a little boy I knew I was doing some things wrong. I always wondered, when I got caught, how did my mother know? Who told on me? So I had some wrong ideas about problems.

There are three wrong attitudes you can have about problems in your life. First, sometimes you may think that because you are a Christian, you should not have problems. Second, you may think you are unspiritual because Christians should not have problems. Third, you may think God has forsaken you because you have problems.

HEALTHY PROBLEM-SOLVING ATTITUDES

Job said, "Man born of a woman has a short life and many problems" (Job 14:1, ELT). So you have problems; your friends have problems; everyone has problems. Since everyone has problems, you cannot run from them.

No one is immune to problems. Everyone is a sinner (see Romans 3:23), they are born that way (see Romans 5:12), and they have a sin nature. They will break laws and do what they are not supposed to do, then not tell the truth, and lie to cover up their mistakes. As a result they will have problems in life, and they will cause you problems.

A healthy approach is knowing you can solve problems. Yes, there are big problems in life; they need a big solution. Also, there are thorny problems with all types of consequences, and it will take time to solve those problems. And yes, there are small problems that must be solved. You can solve them.

WHAT ARE SOME CAUSES OF PROBLEMS?

One of the first causes of problems is change. The Duke of Canterbury said, "Any change for any reason for any purpose is deplorable"—whether that is a change in schedule, or a change in the way you do things, or a change of attitude, or sometimes a new job, new home, new city, new friends, etc. So whenever you go through changes, expect problems.

Differences cause problems. When a man and woman plan to get married, they have to agree on many things during their courtship before marriage. But afterward they find they have differences because of background, or culture, or experiences. It may be the way their parents raised them, or they had different ways of handling problems or difficulties in life. Therefore, when you run into differences with another person, first look for ways you can agree on solving a problem, but don't ignore the differences that can cause problems.

Circumstances can cause problems. Sometimes our problems arise from our personal needs. You may need a new way of doing things, or you may need to find a new store for groceries, new places to find gasoline, or even a new place to buy a new car. Any of these can cause problems in life.

THREE QUESTIONS TO ASK

1. How big is the problem?

When you are facing what you think is a big problem, it might be smaller than you imagine. So a well-defined problem can be a half-solved problem. So ask, "How big is my problem?" What you need is objective eyes to analyze the problem; look at all the details, as well as study the consequences of the problem. That way you can find out the size or the implication your problem may have on your life.

2. Who is involved in the problem?

Most of our problems do not come from circumstances or the things that surround us in life. Most of our problems are conflicts of attitude or ways of doing things. Like it or not, many problems are caused by people. Oh yes, there are house problems, car problems, or things problems. But begin by finding out who is involved with the problem. Your first step in solving a problem is locating its source.

3. What does the larger group think about the problem?

If the problem is between two people in a family, find out what the whole family thinks. If the problem is at work, find out what those at work think. When trying to solve a problem, ask for other people's opinions; you may get their support and help. If many people are involved in the problem, then many people may need to be involved in the solution.

THREE WRONG ATTITUDES TOWARD PROBLEMS

First, you can fuss about the problem. Some people fuss at their spouse, or other family members, or their friends. Fussing about your problems will not solve them, and in many cases it may intensify them.

Second, you can fight your problems by fighting the people who caused the problem—or the organization, or anything, or anyone who caused your problem. Also, sometimes we fight our family, our friends, or complete strangers. But when we resist our problems and the people causing our problems, we no longer are ready to solve them. As a matter of fact, we probably won't solve them.

Third, you can let your problems kill you. This means it kills your incentive to live or work. Also, your problem can kill your home life, work life, or church life. Either your problem will kill you or you can work on it and kill it. However, one or the other needs to take place.

THREE PROBLEM-SOLVING EYES

First, pray for spiritual eyes to see your problem. You can ask God to give you His eyes to see it as He sees it. Then you can ask for God's help: "Lord, increase our faith" (Luke 17:5). When you look at the problem from God's perspective, you may begin to see a solution.

Second, you need eyes to see the people involved. When you find yourself in a problem, look at the people involved. Some people may be instigators of the problem and may or may not be aware they have created the problem. But you need to know who is involved.

Third, you need solution eyes. When approaching a problem, be careful about trying to affix blame or determining who is at fault. Even if you think you know, it might not help to point the finger, or expose them, or blame them. Let your information search speak for itself. Sometimes when you put all the facts on the table, you are not blaming another; the facts speak for themselves. When you lay out the facts, remember that you are focused on a solution—so spend your energy looking for all the possible solutions. Always let the facts speak for themselves.

PROBLEM-SOLVING STEP BY STEP

The following five steps first appeared in print 600 years before Christ was born. Greek philosophers were suggesting how to think, or how to have creative thoughts to solve difficulties, or in the case of this chapter, how to solve problems. These five steps are suggestions to guide you when facing difficulties, unknown territories, or problems.

1. Get the facts.

Before you try to solve a problem, gather as many facts, data, or information about the problem as possible. Go through files, references, lists, and past phone conversations. Do everything you can to get as much information before you try to solve the problem.

Technically you must define a problem before you try to solve a problem. One of the best ways to start—and get the problem out of your mind—is to write the problem or issue out on paper. When you can clearly define a problem for other people to see, that means you also have a clearer understanding of what must be done to solve a problem.

You make good decisions on good information.

You make bad decisions on bad information.

Never make any decision without information.

2. Establish biblical principles.

Remember, principles found in the Bible represent more than a divine revelation on God's intent; the principles of Scripture represent good common sense. So when some will not go to the Bible for answers, or reject the Bible's authority, you can at least get them to look at the problem objectively as you have written it out. That way they can focus on the problem to be solved.

3. Evaluate/study the facts.

By looking/studying/evaluating your data carefully, you may find the cause of the problem. When your problem is written out, others can see the issues objectively. And remember, a well-defined problem is a half-solved problem. By writing out the problem, you get the issue out of everyone's thinking and the problem is separated from people's emotions and ulterior motives. Sometimes the problem may involve family, or sometimes every person in your life. By looking at it objectively, you can separate the problem from any emotional feelings you have. Also remember, your emotions may lead to a snap judgment or a conclusion without or apart from the facts.

4. Determine the various solutions to the problem.

There is always more than one way to solve a problem. So make a list of the various ways that your problem can be solved. Write each one out so you and others can objectively study the proposal. Try to make the list as complete as possible. As you think about the various solutions to the problem, remember that there are many ways a problem can be expressed. By writing out all the possible solutions, you are forcing yourself to think about various solutions and ways of handling the problem.

Remember, God may speak to you through someone else's ideas or your own thoughts, but usually He uses information/facts. So the more information you gather about your problem and the better you express it in many different ways, the easier it will be to solve your problems. After you write out your various solutions and put them in a list, you can better see which solution is best.

5. Choose/apply the best solution.

Remember, you live in an imperfect world and there may be no perfect solutions/conclusions in this life. There are only the best solutions that come from an objective approach to your problem. Now is a good time to yield the problem to God. Ask Him to guide you to an answer; you can also pray for God's wisdom to understand all the facts. Then go a step further in your prayer and pray about each one of the solutions, asking God to lead you to the best solution.

Finally, ask yourself, "What is God teaching me through this process?" Sometimes we face a problem and solve it and never learn lessons from it. After you ask what God wants you to learn, apply the solution to your life.

PRACTICAL PRINCIPLES

1. The weightier your problem, the longer it may take to find a solution.

Because the problem may have many implications and long-range ramifications, your attempt to solve the problem may weigh on you. Therefore, you want as much information as possible, so give yourself time as you gather all the data. The more time you spend in prayer about the problem, the easier it will be to find the correct solution. You might even want to fast, e.g., a one-day fast over the problem.

When the problem has you over the barrel and your thinking is not clear, you must spend more time studying the issues and more time in prayer asking God to lead you to the right solution.

2. Plan Bible reading that deals with your problem.

The Bible is a book about theology, to explain the nature and principles of God's work in the world, but it is a devotional approach to worship and praising God. Also, it is a book of life and you will find that many of the problems you face were faced by people in the Bible. Look at their historical background and how they faced their problems. What were their alternative solutions? You may find going to the Word of God will guide you into the best solution for your problem; it may be God's solution.

3. Obviously you want to pray over the entire problem.

First, ask God to make you as objective as you can be about the problem. Then ask God to help you find in Scripture the information you need. Then pray as you gather data, asking God to give you insight as you evaluate all the facts. Finally, as you move toward a solution, ask God to give the right insight and help you write a clear statement of the solution to your problem.

4. Write and rewrite your problem.

One of the best ways to think is with a pencil or pen at your fingertips. As you write down what you're thinking, you see the problem on paper and you view the issues more objectively. You don't realize it but your emotions influence everything you think. Every word has pluses, and some of them have minuses. These emotional expressions will influence your thinking at all times. But when you write down both the problem and the solution on a sheet of paper, it is there in black in white for you to read, study, and perhaps lead you to a more objective decision.

5. Write out the possible solution before attempting to apply it.

Yes, you have already written down the problem, and you made a list of all the different solutions. But now you want to write out your *step-by-step* approach to solve the problem and how you will approach it. Your expression of the problem on paper will give you insight you have not gained thus far.

6. In your darkest hour, remember that God has an answer/solution.

If God knows the answer to your problem, wouldn't you want to be as close to Him as possible to find His answer? That involves prayer but also meditation and spending time in His presence. That also includes being on talking terms with Him.

Abraham sent Eliezer, his old trusted servant, to go back to Abraham's home on the Tigris-Euphrates river and find a wife for his son Isaac. This was a major task, and whatever choice Eliezer made would determine the future of Abraham's posterity, even the future of God's people. When Eliezer got to Abraham's former home to begin looking at the possibilities for a wife for Isaac, he prayed. See? Even thousands of years ago people approached their problems like you should approach your problems today. Because Eliezer prayed, he testified, "As for me, being on the way, the Lord led me" (Genesis 24:27). He was suggesting that the Lord led him to "Abraham's relatives where he found Rebecca to marry Isaac." God can do for you what He did for Eliezer. But you must pray and wait on God as did Eliezer.

Chapter 2

SUCCESSFUL
PROBLEM-SOLVING

L IFE is about choices, and the choices you make determine who you are, how you live, and your destination in life. Those who make God their choice end up on God's side. That does not mean they will have an easy life. But the choice of God will help and guide you to the answers. Also, satan, the enemy of God, will tempt you and test you. But as you choose God, let Him indwell you, give you power, and lead you to your destination in life.

But those who choose the opposite of God and His will end up with an evil life. It might be an easy or a difficult life, but sin always has consequences. However, many who serve satan in this life have it much easier until death. Then there is another issue. If they are not born again and know Jesus Christ as Savior, they will end up in hell, which is punishment forever.

You must always make the right choice in life—not most of the time, but all of the time. You must make right choices about the most important areas, at the right time, and you will have the most success.

God knows both sides of any choice you will make, so He can give you guidance or warnings. First of all, God has given us the Ten

Commandments, telling us what not to do. We must not serve other gods but serve only the Lord God of Heaven in whose image we are created. We must not make idols or worship them; take God's name in vain; abuse the Lord's Sabbath day; dishonor our parents; murder, commit adultery, steal, lie, or covet/desire things that are not ours.

Note that these Ten Commandments are not suggestions; they are laws, and those who break God's laws suffer the consequences of those laws.

In addition to the Ten Commandments, there are over 600 negative warnings in Scripture that warn the Christian what not to do. What can you learn from these negative warnings? Begin by reading the Word of God, digesting its truth, and living by its directives.

GOD SPELLS OUT POSITIVE RULES

Jesus Christ your Savior lives in your heart and will guide you through the problems of life. First of all, He calls you to follow Him, love Him, and serve Him. "And we know that all things work together for good to those who love God, to those who are the called according to His purpose" (Romans 8:28). And while His love guides us, remember that He does it internally ... directly ... daily ... continually.

Second, God will guide you as you allow Him to control your life: "For as many as are led by the Spirit of God, these are sons of God" (Romans 8:14).

Third, God may direct through opportunities and open doors. Paul told the Corinthians, "For a great and effective door has opened to me" (1 Corinthians 16:9). While Paul was describing certain opportunities to preach the gospel, look at the broader application of that verse. God guides each of us to certain opportunities broader than preaching. He challenges us to take advantage of open doors.

Another way God guides us is through yielding ourselves to Him. Paul tells us "to present your bodies a living sacrifice, holy, acceptable to God, which is your reasonable service" (Romans 12:1). The word "present" actually is to yield, submit, or give control of your body to Jesus Christ. But there is a warning and a promise with this command: "And do not be conformed to this world, but be transformed by the renewing of your mind, that you may prove what *is* that good and acceptable and perfect will of God" (Romans 12:2).

So, when you give yourself to God, you make a decision to not give yourself to sin, or evil, or things that are contrary to God's plan for holy living. When you obey God, He blesses you, uses you, and enriches you.

Next, God directs you through your spiritual gifts and/or abilities. Everyone is given spiritual strengths or abilities; these are also called strength of character, strength of ability, or strength of personality. Paul said, "But each one has his own gift from God" (1 Corinthians 7:7).

At another place we will examine the spiritual gifts that are given to all believers. Yours may be preaching, or serving, or teaching, or counseling individuals. Therefore, find your strength, i.e., your gift; then find a place to exercise it, and then a place to use it for the glory of God.

God also has given to each of us common sense; this is insight, or understanding, or practical knowledge so that we can approach and solve our problems. The Bible describes God's role in our common sense: "A man's heart plans his way, but the Lord directs his steps" (Proverbs 16:9). In this verse the word "plans" means thinking ahead, analyzing all data, and planning a conclusion.

The wrong decision at the wrong time—disaster

The wrong decision at the right time—mistake

The right decision at the wrong time—unacceptable

The right decision at the right time—success

10 PRINCIPLES FOR MAKING SUCCESSFUL DECISIONS

As you study the following 10 suggestions, ask yourself how often you use each of these suggestions. Try to put them in order of importance to you. How have each given you direction, and how have you used them?

1. Take time to listen to God's voice.

Before you make a decision, pray about the issues on each side of the decision, asking God to give you insight and leadership as you continue studying your options. Then pray about each of the solutions you may use. As you pray and meditate, God can lead you to the right decision. When God says, "Be still, and know that I am God" (Psalm 46:10), He is telling you to first listen to Him as a way to live.

2. Ask and answer questions about yourself (because God asks questions).

When Adam and Eve sinned by eating what God had told them not to eat, God came to them with a question: "Adam, where are you?" (Genesis 3:9).

The next story in the Bible tells of Cain killing his brother Abel. Obviously this is the first murder. Cain tried to run away, but God came to him with a question: "Cain, why are you angry?" (Genesis 4:6).

Remember when Paul was a Pharisee fighting the Christian church? He was on his way to Damascus to arrest Christians and bring them to Jerusalem. It was then that God stopped him, blinding him with a blinding light. It was then that Paul asked, "Who are you, Lord?" (Acts 9:5). Learn to ask and answer questions, and get solutions to problems.

3. Recognize objective truth.

We should all recognize the existence of facts—facts are facts. We recognize them in the dictionary, encyclopedia, and other books of knowledge. So it is difficult to know how to approach a problem, or how to solve a problem, or even the next step.

Remember, sometimes God's answer is loud; you cannot miss His directions. You can read your answer in Scripture, or you can find it in other places. And other times God's voice is a "still small voice"—so quiet that it seems God is silent. So what do you do? Truth is like gravity; it is always there and you cannot deny its existence. It takes time, patience, and persistence, but you can find truth.

4. Stop self-effort and yield to God.

Now, self-effort includes trying to think of an answer, searching for an answer, or relying on your memory. But if you yield to God, putting your mind in neutral, you are waiting for God to speak to you. "And whatever you do in word or deed, *do* all in the name of the Lord Jesus, giving thanks to God the Father through Him" (Colossians 3:17).

5. Know the difference between a physical response and a mental understanding.

When you are facing a problem and you are pressing to think your way to an answer, make sure your physical body is not speaking so loudly that you cannot hear yourself think. Sometimes your body speaks so loudly—demands attention because it is hungry, tired, angry, etc.; then it is time to shut down the body so you can listen to your mind.

6. Pay attention to your spiritual nature.

This is an interesting point. We should all pay attention to our spiritual nature all the time. But we don't. First, we should yield to God like Paul had to do. When Paul was confronted by Jesus on the road to Damascus, he asked, "Lord, what would You have me to do?" (Acts 9:6). That is a great question for you to ask the Lord when facing a problem.

Second, search with your whole heart. Sometimes we let our previous thoughts or our memory control us. But if you are searching for the truth—the whole truth—or you are searching for God, then "You will seek Me and find Me, when you search your whole heart" (Jeremiah 29:13).

Third, allow God to search you and ask questions. When God asks questions, you had better listen. Also, when God asks questions, He wants answers. "I the Lord search the heart" (Jeremiah 17:10).

Fourth, let the Holy Spirit guide your thinking. Remember, the Holy Spirit was given to us for this purpose. "The Holy Spirit ... will teach you all things and bring all things to your remembrance" (John 14:26).

Fifth, study. Yes, you are going to study the Scriptures, but you want to study all things related to your problem. You may have to look in a Bible dictionary or a Bible encyclopedia, or you may go to some reference books to find the answer. However, do not forget to search the Bible. "Study to shew thyself approved unto God, a workman that needeth not to be ashamed, rightly dividing the word of truth" (2 Timothy 2:15, KJV).

Sixth, search in prayer on your knees before God. In one sense, you must search the Bible for the answer. But in another sense, you must search the mind of God. But in a final sense, you must let God search you. "Search me O God" (Psalm 139:23). You may not like what God finds in your heart, but it is better for Him to find it and reveal it than for any problem in your life to go unsolved or any potential danger to be undiscovered.

7. Obey what you learn.

When you start searching for truth, make sure you find it, examine it, then begin to apply it to your life. But finally, make sure you obey it. When Paul found the truth, he could say, "I was not disobedient" (Acts 26:19).

8. Be patient.

Sometimes the answer you want does not come immediately. It may take extra research, and it may take extra thought. The more you search for the answer, the more data you will dig up—and more data is like light that shines on the problem to give you the answer. Sometimes God speaks slowly, like the dawning of a new day. When the light first comes over the eastern horizon every morning, you know the sun is coming, even when you cannot see it. But you know it will be a bright day even when it is still dusk outside. Whatever you need, be patient, because the sun is coming.

9. Be open to insight from others.

Sometimes we get locked into our own thinking and we find ourselves in jail. So be ready to learn from others. How do you do that? By asking them, listening to them, questioning them, and then together you and the other person seek the right answer. Remember that at Paul's conversion, God sent Ananias to help his blindness. Ananias said, "Brother Saul ... God has sent me ... receive your sight" (Acts 9:17).

10. Be prepared to be misunderstood.

Sometimes when you get the answer, you know the answer is right but no one else agrees with you. Be prepared to be misunderstood. Remember, Paul, on the road to Damascus, saw a bright light that blinded him. He saw Jesus, and that light transformed his life. Those traveling with him did not understand because they did not see the light, nor did they understand Jesus speaking to Paul. They only heard a voice speaking in a foreign language. They did not see Jesus. God did not speak to them. They did not understand what was going on.

Chapter 3

A STUDY OF GOOD AND BAD CHOICES

TO see bad choices, all you have to do is look at the history for them. You might even look in the rearview mirror of your life to see some of the bad choices you made. What would you do differently if you were given the opportunity again? However, would you have enough information to do it differently if given the opportunity again?

WHY PEOPLE MAKE POOR CHOICES

1. They guess because they don't know the answer.

When people don't have enough information, sometimes they run ahead and guess the answer. But if they are wrong, and if they act on that choice, they make a mistake.

2. People get bad information.

If people don't know what the correct information is, nor do they know the truth, then what else can they do but make bad choices?

People make good choices on good information.

People make bad choices on bad information.

Without any information, they make lucky choices.

Some have good luck; some have bad luck.

3. Many people never learned how to make good decisions.

They are always quick to make snap decisions. Sometimes they are right and sometimes they are wrong. Perhaps they are impatient and do not take the time to study the things that cause the problem, so they cannot make a good decision about the problem.

4. Perhaps they have developed a pattern of wrong decisions over the years.

And that pattern has become a habit, and therefore they continue to make bad decisions because they have always made bad decisions. Sometimes it is not the final decision they make but the process. They have never learned the right process, and they never study carefully how to make good decisions.

5. Their hero made wrong decisions.

As a young boy I lived through World War II and I saw the bad decisions that Hitler, Chancellor of Germany, made that thrust all of Europe into a war. Based on what Adolf Hitler did, many of his generals made the same bad decisions, as well as other military leaders down the line. Those bad decisions led to their death, the destruction of Germany and other nations, as well as the death of people on both sides of the issue.

If your spiritual leader makes a bad decision, be careful that you don't make that same decision. Just as your hero and spiritual leader are responsible to God, you are also responsible to God for your decisions.

6. They listen to wrong counselors or advice.

The book of Proverbs tells us, "The advice of the wicked is treacherous" (Proverbs 12:5, NLT). King Rehoboam followed Solomon as king over all of Israel, and 2 Chronicles tells the story of two groups of men trying to advise Rehoboam how to lead the kingdom. The young elders told him, "Your father made our yoke heavy; now therefore, lighten the burdensome service ... and we will serve you" (2 Chronicles 10:4). However, those younger advisers gave him the wrong advice. As a result, Rehoboam said, "Yes, my father laid heavy burdens on you, but I'm going to make them even heavier! My father beat you with whips, but I will beat you with scorpions!" (2 Chronicles 10:11, NLT). How treacherous is bad advice? Rehoboam listened to the bad advice of young men and his nature rebelled against him and he lost half his kingdom.

7. They are headed in the wrong direction.

When people are going the wrong way, don't join them—even better, do not listen to them.

The wrong decision when going the wrong way—disaster

The wrong decision when going the right way—mistake

The right decision at the wrong time—unacceptable

The right decision at the right time—success

8. They don't know their limitations.

Many times, people make a decision about their life but they don't know their limitations. It could be academic, financial, or just their level of experience when faced with a broad responsibility. Some people want to be a college president but they cannot pass a basic freshman college course.

9. They don't know the circumstances.

Sometimes it is difficult to make a decision when you do not know all the circumstances, e.g., the data, facts, public opinion, as well as background.

Years ago, I was visiting the Midwest and talked to a young man who was planning to go to a Bible college to study for the ministry. I was not impressed with the Bible college he mentioned, and I did not want to say anything. But I had heard a rumor that the college was going bankrupt and might not make it through the coming semester.

When the man asked me what he should do, I gave him the following advice: "Talk to your pastor, someone who has graduated from that college, and even someone at the college itself. Ask them if the college will make it financially through the coming year."

I did not tell the young man what to do. I gave him information so that he could make the right decision with his life.

10. Some Christians are ignorant of their spiritual gift.

God has given to each Christian a personality, and with that a spiritual ability—called a spiritual gift—an ability to serve God. Use your spiritual gift to help you know what is the best decision for you.

11. Some Christians do not know how to
find the will of God for their life.

Remember, God has a will for your life and that is called "the perfect will of God" (Romans 12:1). God has a perfect will; but can you stay in His perfect will if you marry the wrong person, or if you don't seek education to prepare for the ministry where God has called you to preach? Some Christians make poor choices because they don't know how to find the will of God.

SUMMARY

In this chapter, a decision is a one-time selection you have to make about life. You should be careful about all of your *decisions* and pray that each one will be correct and right. However, a *selection* involves choices with a number of options and may involve one or more decisions or a one-time choice. So what does that mean to you? You may make one bad decision, but pray that you do not make a bad choice, because a bad choice involves many decisions that lead to a larger direction in life.

WHAT INFLUENCE DOES SIN HAVE ON CHOICES?

Do not love the world or the things in the world. If anyone loves the world, the love of the Father is not in him. For all that is in the world—the lust of the flesh, the lust of the eyes, and the pride of life—is not of the Father but is of the world. (1 John 2:15-16)

1. The lust of the flesh is fulfilling bodily desires or passions.

When the Bible condemns the "lust of the flesh," is it not condemning the normal physical needs that everyone has? We must breathe, we must eat, and we must look after the body to make sure it is healthy, which includes exercise, cleansing, and a proper diet.

When the Bible speaks about the lust of the flesh, it is talking about illicit desires that are condemned in the Bible. These are seen in the Ten Commandments and other places where the Bible condemns living to please the lust of the flesh. This would include illicit sex, drug addiction, alcohol, and other forms of bodily abuses.

You want to pray for God to give you a strong healthy body, so eat healthy, exercise, and get enough sleep to keep yourself in good physical condition. That way you can serve the Lord with a healthy body.

2. The "lust of the eyes" are things that we see and desire but should not have.

The Bible condemns the lust of the eyes. It is telling us to avoid evil pleasures, evil activities, and evil itself. Make sure you understand the difference between normal eyesight and eyes that lust after that which is evil. God gives us eyes so we can see to learn, see to serve, and see to live. We need eyes to serve God and to grow to maturity in Jesus Christ.

However, not everything your eyes see you should desire. And not everything your eyes want you should seek. Be careful about making money your aim in life; you need money to take care of your needs, but that is not the purpose of your life. "For me to live is Christ, and to die is gain" (Philippians 1:21).

Be careful that you do not fix your eyes on stuff ... things ... gadgets ... or things that your neighbor has that you want. In another place we are told, "You shalt not covet [with your eyes] your neighbor's house" (Exodus 20:17, KJV).

3. The pride of life is exalting yourself beyond who you are, and/or beyond what is legal, and/or beyond what God wants for you.

Pride is when you focus everything on yourself and you forget about God, your family, others, and life itself. Pride is seeking to be something you are not and seeking to have something you do not possess. It is seeking power, position, control of others, self-glory, or self-exhortation.

There is a place to have self-respect and self-confidence and even self-acceptance. We should respect ourselves for who we are, not more than we have obtained, and not greater than what we have accomplished. There is a place for a healthy personality with healthy self-respect.

PEOPLE WHO MADE BAD CHOICES

The Bible tells of Lot making bad choices and ending up far from the center of God's blessings. The Bible says, "He chose the well-watered plains of Sodom" (Genesis 13:10). When he did that, he eventually lost his wife, his family, and all the things that mattered to him.

Samson chose women, a certain kind of woman who could satisfy his sexual appetite. As a result of his bad choices, Samson lost his reputation, the opportunity to serve God, and ultimately his life (see Judges 16:1-31).

Achan was one of the leaders who went in with Joshua to capture Jericho. But when he got into the city, he was tempted with lust and made bad choices. "When I saw among the spoils a beautiful Babylonian garment, two hundred shekels of silver, and a wedge of gold weighing fifty shekels, I coveted them and took them" (Joshua 7:21). As a result of stealing and bringing condemnation on the people of God, Achan was stoned to death.

The rich young ruler came to talk with Jesus. He asked the question "what shall I do to inherit eternal life?" (Luke 18:18). The Lord reminded him that he would have to follow the Ten Commandments. The young man claimed he had kept all of them from his youth. "Then Jesus, looking at him, loved him, and said to him, 'One thing you lack: Go your way, sell whatever you have and give to the poor, and you will have treasure in heaven; and come, take up the cross, and follow Me'" (Mark 10:21). This young man made a bad choice: "At this the man's face fell, and he went away sad, for he had many possessions" (Mark 10:22).

Demas was one of the disciples who followed Jesus and worked with Paul. Yet Demas made a choice for a worldly lifestyle. Paul said of him, "Demas has forsaken me, having loved this present world" (2 Timothy 4:10).

PEOPLE WHO MADE GOOD CHOICES

At the beginning of Joshua's ministry, he chose to follow the Lord and was obedient to Moses as they led Israel through the wilderness. When Moses died, Joshua became the leader and led God's people from one victory to another till they conquered the entire Promised Land. Then Joshua could say to everyone, "[C]hoose for yourselves this day whom you will serve, ... But as for me and my house, we will serve the Lord" (Joshua 24:15). Joshua wanted everyone to make the same decision that he had made. He wanted everyone to put God first.

Ruth made a good choice. When Ruth and Orpah were joining Naomi to leave Moab to return to the Promised Land, both Ruth and Orpah could look across the Jordan Valley to see Israel on the other side and its well-watered plains. Also, Orpah could look back and see her friends, her family heritage. She chose not to go with Ruth but to stay in Moab.

Ruth made a choice to follow God. Even when she was told to turn back, Ruth said, "Entreat me not to leave you, or to turn back from following after you; for wherever you go, I will go; and wherever you lodge, I will lodge; your people shall be my people, and your God, my God. Where you die, I will die, and there will I be buried" (Ruth 1:16-17). The most important thing about Ruth is that she chose right, when no one encouraged her and no one supported her decision. But she chose God, and because of that she would be remembered for her good choice, for what she did for God, and for the cause of God's people.

No one knew that Esther was a Hebrew, but she had married the king of Persia, and now she faced the choice to go tell Ahasuerus about the threat to liquidate her and her people Israel.

If Esther stayed quiet, she could save her life. No one knew she was a Jew and she might have been killed when all the other Jews would have been killed. And if she went to tell the king, she could be killed. But she chose right: "if I perish, I perish!" (Esther 4:16).

Solomon showed wisdom. When God appeared to Solomon as he was dreaming at a place called Gibeon, the Lord said to him, "Ask! What shall I give you?" (1 Kings 3:5). That was a wide-open invitation for Solomon to ask for many things. He could have asked for his enemy, wealth, glory, or many other things. Solomon said, "'Therefore give to Your servant an understanding heart to judge Your people, that I may discern between good and evil' ... The speech pleased the Lord ... Then God said to him: 'Because you have asked this thing, and have not asked long life for yourself, nor have asked riches for yourself, nor have asked the life of your enemies, but have asked for yourself understanding to discern justice, behold ... I have given you a wise and understanding heart, so that there has not been anyone like you before you, nor shall any like you arise after you'" (1 Kings 3:9-12).

Chapter 4

HOW TO MAKE GOOD CHOICES FOR YOUR LIFE

WHAT is "choice"? Webster says, (1) Choice is an act of choosing or selecting. (2) The power of choosing. (3) The person or thing chosen. (4) The abundance and variety from which to choose, i.e., a wide choice of options. (5) That which is preferred or desired, i.e., the best or desirable. (6) An alternative. (7) Worthy of being chosen, i.e., excellent, superior. (8) Choice implies the opportunity of making a decision between at least two options. Usually, choice is a free right or privilege that can be exercised at will.

DESCRIPTION OF CHOICES

1. The act of choosing

This is the power or option of one who has the privilege of making a choice: e.g., do I choose steak or hot dog from the menu?

2. The power of choice

Because you have been given the option or privilege of making a choice, you now have the right or option of making a choice based on what you know or desire, or that which would please you or be best for you.

3. The thing chosen

This could be a wide variety of objects, such as food, clothes, housing, vehicle, or your career.

4. The variety on which your decision is made

There are usually many choices in life, not just a decision between two options. In life there are many choices, which makes it all the more difficult to make the right choice.

SOME YES CHOICES ARE ALREADY MADE

1. You cannot choose to worship idols.

God has said, "Thou shalt have no other gods before Me" (Exodus 20:3). Therefore, not only can you not have another god, but you also cannot put *anything* before God. You cannot put anything equal to God. You cannot even give another god any place in your life. If you want to choose God, you can have nothing to do with idols.

2. You cannot choose to use God's name in vain.

"For the Lord will not hold him guiltless" (Exodus 20:3). Some people use God's name in a curse because of habit, and that is wrong. You do not have the privilege of cursing. Some people do it in anger; again that is not a right you can exercise. Other people will use God's name in excitement, but they use it frivolously and wrongly. But then again there is always social pressure. Some people curse and use God's name in vain because of their friends and others around them who are cursing. But God has already made the choice for you; you cannot choose to use His name in vain.

3. You do not have the choice of staying home on the Lord's Day and not worshipping corporately with other believers.

God told His people in the Old Testament to "keep the Sabbath ... to the Lord" (Deuteronomy 5:12, KJV). This is one of the Ten Commandments, and you cannot choose to not worship God on His day. Even the New Testament says, "Don't neglect gathering to worship" (Hebrews 10:25, ELT).

4. You cannot choose to kill someone, steal what does not belong to you, lie, covet, or commit adultery (see Exodus 20:13-17).

God has prohibited these things, so you should not even desire to do these things, think about doing them, or even contemplate doing them. Obviously, you cannot decide to do any of those things. God has already made that choice for you.

THE YES CHOICE FOR GOOD

1. You need to be involved in the Great Commission.

Jesus gave the command to "go into all the world and preach the gospel to every person" (Matthew 28:19). You cannot choose to ignore God's initiative. He has commanded us to go and to preach; every person in the world must hear. You may not be able to go yourself, but your church must support those who are going, and you personally must support your church by praying, encouraging, and financially supporting world evangelism.

2. You must support God's work with your financial offerings.

When God gives a command, "bring all the tithes into the storehouse" (Malachi 3:10), you cannot choose not to give to God. That choice has already been made. You are to bring one-tenth of what you have and give to God. This could be from your salary, or bonus, or even a gift of money. God has already made the choice whether you should bring gifts to Him or not. Note quickly, God does not tell you how much; it is just that you must give a percentage of what you have.

---

3. You must know and always choose to obey
    God and do what He has told you to do.

You don't have the privilege of refusing God or telling Him no. The author of Hebrews tells us, "[D]o not refuse Him who speaks" (Hebrews 12:25). If you harden your heart and refuse to do what God tells you to do, His voice will get fainter and fainter until you do not hear Him at all.

Also, it is possible to drown out God's voice with voices from other people, entertainment, amusements, and any other attractions in life.

So what does God tell you about making choices? "We must give the more earnest heed to the things we have heard, lest we drift away" (Hebrews 2:1). Every time you make a positive yes to God, the next time He speaks to you, you will hear Him more clearly. Also, every time you make a positive yes to God, you make the next decision even easier.

CHOICES YOU DID NOT MAKE

Think of all the choices in life that involved you but you never had a chance to make those decisions. You are what you are today, you do what you do today, and you know where you want to go probably because of someone else's choices.

1. Your parents determined your
    finances and outlook in life.

As a mother and father train their children about money, decisions, and life, they not only mold their children's values and attitudes, but they also sharpen their children's visions of life of what they want to be and do.

2. Your culture forms your natural values and attitudes.

Whether you grew up in Indiana, China, New York, or Russia, the culture in which you grew up forms your values and focuses your ideals. You did not choose your parents, nor your culture, nor the social/economic structure of society you wanted. That means you did not choose to be rich, average, or poor.

3. Your gender guides many of your physical decisions.

If you are a boy, many decisions are made for you: where you go to the bathroom, what kind of clothes you wear, and how you will preform in life—maybe even the sports you play, the job you have, and how you live. The same can be said for a girl. Those decisions are made by your gender at birth.

4. Your relatives will influence you, including brothers, sisters, aunts, and uncles.

They all have some influence on your life. While they may not control you, cannot make you do all that you do, and will not determine all that you can become, they still will influence you.

5. God chose you before you chose Him.

The Bible says, "He [God] chose us in Him before the foundation of the world" (Ephesians 1:4). Whether you like it or not, God loves you, has a plan for your life, has chosen you, and wants to give you a good life and use you in His ministry.

6. Christ died for you before you
asked Him to be your Savior.

Jesus is "the Lamb slain from the foundation of the world" (Revelation 13:8). He died for you; now you must believe in Him for salvation.

14 LIFE-CHANGING DECISIONS YOU MUST MAKE

1. Salvation

Whether you like it or not, God chose you before the foundation of world. Jesus said, "You have not chosen Me, but I have chosen you" (John 15:15). Yet, because God chose you, you have to choose Him and choose salvation. You have to ask Christ to come into your heart. Your choice must reflect Joshua's challenge: "choose you this day whom ye will serve" (Joshua 24:15, KJV).

2. Whether to be holy and separate from evil

We are exhorted to live holy lives, not to give ourselves to sin. We are warned about the consequences of evil living, and we are challenged with the rewards that God has for pure living. Paul writes, "I plead with you to give your bodies to God ... as a living and holy sacrifice" (Romans 12:1, NLT).

3. Marriage

America is not a society of forced marriages; marriage is a choice between a man and a woman. But look at the choice carefully; it usually involves choosing the type of lifestyle you will have after marriage, because that will be determined by you and your spouse. But your choice that you make usually reflects your inner values and attitudes, so it becomes a prediction of who you will become after marriage.

4. Occupation

Technically you choose the job you want. However, sometimes when you start majoring in a certain vocation in high school or college, you end up in that job once you graduate. Or you come from a family that has always been carpenters, or railway engineers. Sometimes that pressure forces you into that job. But in another sense, a job chooses you. When you look at all the things that you could do to make a living, all the things you could do to spend your life, sometimes you choose a job for what it offers you, and therefore the job chooses you.

5. Education

Like it or not, in America you can choose how smart you want to be. Children are given an opportunity to get an education from first grade to high school graduation. The opportunity is there; what the person chooses to do with that opportunity determines what they are going to become in life. So education is a choice. A young girl can do well and make the honor roll and excel in life. A young boy can hate school, flunk out, and end up with a job that pays minimum wage. Yes, life is a choice.

6. Faithfulness to God

You choose how diligently you will follow Christ and how diligently you will serve Him in this life. Faithfulness to God is a choice. But it is not about faithfulness; it is about God Himself. God promised that "those who seek me diligently will find me" (Proverbs 8:17).

7. Whether to have a clean mind and body

Many children pick up the habit of cursing very young, and it is hard to break it in life. Since words are an expression of the inner person, how they express their words is really an expression of who they are and what they want people to think of them. Those who curse do so for selfish reasons, and they want people to think of them with a certain evil slant. So choose not to curse, and be identified with God and have speech that will glorify God.

8. What kinds of friends we will have

Usually, we choose friends who like us and we like them. But you will be influenced to become like your friends, so your choice of friends determines your life. Proverbs tells us, "As iron sharpens iron, so a man sharpens the countenance of his friend" (Proverbs 27:17). Therefore, our friends are a reflection of how we look at life, what we value most, and what contribution we want to make. If your friends are not lifting you up, then where are you heading?

9. To be a happy or angry person

Some people go through life with a smile, some men always want to whistle, and other people may have a twinkle in their eye. They seem to always be happy, even though there could be sad moments and difficulties in life. But are they happy because they choose to be happy? Other people seem to be angry and always mad at people. You can hear it in their tone of voice, their questions are sharp, and their response is usually belligerent. Proverbs tells us that "happy is the man that findeth wisdom" (Proverbs 3:13, KJV).

10. Whether to be an obedient Christian or to walk on the edge of Christianity

Some people are always curious about what is on the other side, i.e., the evil side of life. So they walk as close to the edge to see what life is like, whether it is X-rated films, or illicit sex, or some other pastime that does not lift them up to God. Perhaps it is inward rebellion and strong-headed will that makes some people turn against God. They ignore the church and will not listen as you share the message of Jesus Christ. People have chosen whether they will be obedient and walk close to God, or close to the edge.

11. What appearance we will make

There are some people who are always neat in their dress, because they have chosen to be that way. They would not think of wearing dirty clothes, the same with wrinkles and worn-out clothes. They want that clean, crisp appearance in life. Other people seem to always be grungy or dirty. Why is that? Because they are comfortable that way. They want to live life in the comfort zone and they choose to be unkempt.

12. How to react to failure and success

No one can control what happens to them, but they can control what happens in them. You cannot control whether you will be successful, but you can control how you will respond to failure, as well as how you will respond to success. The one who responds positively to success and seeks success will probably be successful in life. The one who always lets failure control their life may have been hurt and wants people to know why/where they are hurt, and they show it.

13. How we will serve the Lord

God wants people to serve Him. How you choose to serve the Lord determines what kind of person you will be, what kind of life you will live, and the level of living. If you are serving God, then Christ is the center of your life. You have the attitude "I can do all things through Christ who strengthens me" (Philippians 4:13).

14. Where we live

Most choices of where we live in life are made by our income, our occupation, our self-perception of importance, sometimes by our spouse, and other times God leads us to a certain place to live. Where you live may be your choice, but then again, other factors may influence that choice. You may live where you don't want to live. You may want to live at the beach, or on the golf course, but you live in an apartment building on the fifteenth floor, and you catch a bus to work each day.

Chapter 5

MAKING CHOICES WITH GOD'S HELP

THERE will always be choices in life, and you will always face them. Why? Because there will always be problems. Where do you begin when facing choices? First, realize God has a plan or purpose for your life. "I have a plan for your life, for good and not evil" (Jeremiah 29:11, ELT).

If God has a plan for your life, then He will not hide it from you, because He is a good God. Since God has a plan for your life, He will find ways to show it to you, because He is a wise God. Now that you believe God has a plan for your life, He will make sure you find it.

When you realize God has a plan for your life, you must also realize He wants you to make right choices as you fulfill/complete that plan. Paul reminds us about making right choices: "Let God transform you into a new person by changing the way you think. Then you will learn to know God's will for you, which is good and pleasing and perfect" (Romans 12:2, NLT).

God not only wants you to be concerned about choices, but He also wants you to be concerned about every big choice as well as every small choice. Therefore, you want to make the correct choice about both big and small choices, and make sure you approach them in the right way/attitude to make the right decision every time.

Big choices determine your destiny; therefore, spend quality prayer time about those big choices. Also, spend time examining those choices, then pray about them as much as possible—to make the best choices.

However, there are many little choices in life that are just as important as big choices because little choices make a big difference. And what difference do they make? Little choices determine your character. These choices show up by being on time, not wasting money, showing appreciation to others, saying thank you, doing the best you can with every job that you do.

Remember, there are no little choices in eternity. Every choice you make involving eternity has eternal implications, so make sure that you always make the right choices.

Live a life yielded to God so that your primary concern is always God's concern. Always ask yourself the question, what would Jesus do? Remember the Scriptures: "Christ ... left us an example that we should follow His step" (1 Peter 2:21, ELT).

Even with the above advice, many still do not know what to do. They are like Paul, who responded as he did when asked if he would live or die: "what to choose, I know not" (Philippians 1:22, ELT).

HELP TO FIND AND MAKE GOD'S CHOICE

Who are those who fear the Lord? He will show them the path they should choose. (Psalm 25:12, NLT)

1. Good choices are consistent with the Word of God.

You may not always verify your choice by a Bible verse or a reference from Scripture, but all choices should be made in keeping with biblical truth. So what does that mean? Don't make choices contrary to what the Bible says or what you know is right. It is always right to tell the truth; therefore it is wrong to lie. It is always right to honor the Lord with your speech; therefore it is wrong to curse or use God's name in vain. It is always right to honor the life of others and the life of everyone else; therefore it is wrong to kill. Therefore "choose what is right, and reject what is wrong" (Isaiah 7:16, NLT).

Follow positive principles in your life. Meditate on Scripture and let God's Word influence your thinking. Pray for God's guidance and let Him lead you through your choices.

So when it comes to some choices, the Bible may not tell you what choice you should make, it will not tell what to do on many occasions, but it will give you a context in which to make choices. And what is context? It's your attitude, positive relationships, and purpose in life.

So when it comes to making choices consistent with the Word of God, you will find that the Bible gives you a guide for living. Notice what the psalmist said: "I am determined to obey You until I die" (Psalm 119:112, TLB).

2. Prayer guides you into right choices.

You cannot always stop to pray about every choice, but you can pray every day that God will guide you to make all choices according to His will. Accept this motto and direction in life: "Seek first the kingdom of God" (Matthew 6:33).

However, you will want to pray constantly about all the major, or big, choices you face in life. This may be your choice about a mate in marriage, a job, a major in college, or any other choice that will determine your life's direction.

And while praying, ask God to slowly conform you into the image of God so you can become like Jesus Christ. With that influence, you will make better decisions.

Therefore, when praying about choices, sometimes it is best to wait before making a choice. God may be doing His work as you wait for Him. So let circumstances or occasions develop as you pray. The writer of Proverbs said that as we wait and pray about long-range plans, we can have the assurance God will guide each step we take. "We can make our plans, but the Lord determines our steps" (Proverbs 16:9, NLT).

3. Make all choices in view of God's work in your life.

One of the key verses to use in asking for God's direction is "not as I will, but as thou wilt" (Matthew 26:39, KJV). When you yield yourself to God and wait for Him to guide you as you make a decision, you can be sure God is working.

Be careful of fighting God when He is trying to tell you what to do. If you are resisting the will of God, what you don't want to do may be God's will. So examine your heart and intentions to determine if you are resisting what God is telling you to do.

On the other hand, when you are yielded to God and you walk through life with a yielded spirit, what you want to do may be God's will.

4. Make choices in view of your strength and spiritual giftedness.

Before you have to make a choice when facing a problem, determine your inner strength of character. That involves finding your spiritual giftedness and spiritual strength. So find your spiritual gift, use your spiritual gift, and plan to live according to your strengths. "Each man has a special gift from God" (1 Corinthians 7:7, NLT).

Especially examine your spiritual gift in light of full-time Christian service. God did not plan for everyone to be in full-time Christian ministry. The Bible gives many illustrations of laymen who are used of God to carry out His will. Therefore, whether you are a layman/laywoman or in full-time ministry, find your spiritual gift and determine how it operates in your life. Don't let guilt push you into full-time Christian service. Only go there if God is calling you.

Now for all others not in full-time Christian service, follow your strong, positive desire to serve Him and then your spiritual gifts can be used in ministry.

Look at it this way: God wants everyone to serve Him full time, all the time, in all ways possible. But that does not mean you are in full-time ministry being supported by wages for your ministry. So begin by finding your spiritual gift. Remember, "Everyone has his own particular gift from God" (1 Corinthians 7:7, Phillips).

5. Listen to counsel from mature family and friends when making choices.

Usually family and friends are those who love you, want the best for you, and will pray for you. Therefore, listen when these people give you good advice—biblical advice—so that you are glorifying and serving the Lord. Remember, "plans go wrong from lack of advice" (Proverbs 15:22, NLT).

Here is another reason to listen to advice and direction from friends: "In the multitude of counselors, there is safety" (Proverbs 11:14). Why? Because they can keep you from harm and they want you to live and minister safely. They usually see the issues more objectively than you do. When they explain a situation to you, perhaps you can see things through their perspective, and you will see God's will through their eyes.

Another thing, those friends and counselors will make you think about the consequences that lie on the other side of bad choices. These are things that you may not force yourself to think about. They can save you from consequences you might have faced. Our friends who love us and want the best for us will warn us about bad decisions.

One of the questions that can be asked when seeking counsel is, what would Jesus do? Now we don't always know exactly how Jesus would react, nor what He would do, but when we are aware of the opinion He might have, we can make better decisions.

6. The right choice may be found by common sense.

When using the term "common sense," we need a definition. Common sense is sound judgment in practical matters, or a basic human ability to understand and guide oneself. Here is an old adage to describe it: "Don't get God mad by breaking His Ten Commandments."

Therefore, only seldom will God lead contrary to common sense, because common sense usually expresses the laws of the universe. Since God created those laws when He put the universe in its place, His law reflects common sense. So don't break His laws. Also, common sense is treating other people right because God created people and made them in His image. Therefore, check all your decisions with Scripture.

7. The right choices can be found through positive circumstances.

In the Bible this is sometimes called the open door of opportunity. Paul tells us, "There is a wide-open door for a great work here" (1 Corinthians 16:9, NLT). Therefore, Paul saw a great opportunity to do ministry for God to carry out the Great Commission. He did not have to pray about it, nor did he have to examine the circumstances or even ask his friends what to do. The opportunity was an open door for Paul to walk through.

At the same time, a closed door can give you a negative assurance in decision-making. When you apply for a job and you get a no, that could be assurance for you to look elsewhere. The same when a man asks a woman to marry him and she says no; that could be an emotional assurance to move on.

Just one more thing: when you have already made a bad choice and you know it, what can you do? Examine how you made the choice, asking why you did it. Ask yourself what you would do the next time. By examining and understanding bad choices, you can have a positive approach to a constructive future life and choices.

8. God shows His will to those who are actively serving and seeking His will.

Look at a sailboat out on the water. The direction of the sail determines whether the boat will move forward rapidly with the wind, move slowly in a cross wind, or stop because it is fighting the wind. The answer? The set of the sail determines the direction and speed of the boat. In the same way, when you choose to do God's will, that is like setting the sails of a boat to always choose to do right, always asking God to give direction, and letting God determine the speed of the boat of your life. When you have set the sail properly, you will determine the direction of your life.

WHAT IS GOD'S BLUEPRINT
FOR YOUR LIFE?

1. A blueprint

In one sense your life is like a blueprint, but God is the architect/engineer who has drawn the blueprint for your life. He knows what plans He has for you, what He wants you to do, and how He will use you. In that sense, all choices have been made for you, and your main purpose is to find God's will and do God's will. This way you glorify Him and can be used by Him.

But what if you make wrong choices that were not God's will? Sometimes you disobey God and sin against Him. You find yourself outside God's will. You end up in places, positions, and connected to people that are contrary to God's will. What then? When you come back into His will, you may not have His perfect will because you messed that up. Your next choice may venture into an area known as God's permissive will. Here you may not have God's previous will for your life but still God has a new plan for your life. He makes a new plan for your life based on the poor decisions—or wrong decisions. When you do this, you may find yourself living on the edge of new possibilities rather than in God's original plan for your life. However, no matter who you are, or where you are, God can use you, guide you, and make your life profitable.

2. God's will is a compass.

When you look at a compass, you can't change the needle; it always points in the same direction, i.e., it points north. Therefore, when you come to the Word of God, it will always point you toward God, toward righteousness, and toward His will. Therefore, the Bible is like a compass that will always point you toward God, so direct your life by the compass of God's Word.

When you are lost in the woods, you look to your compass to find out which way is north. Then you know which way to go. So if you want to go north, follow the point of the compass needle. If you want to do right, follow the needle of the Word of God.

You will never be in the wrong place when you follow the Word of God, but rather, when your life centers on God's Word, you are in the center of God's will.

PART TWO

FAITH
WALKING
through
PROBLEMS

DEVOTIONS

Day 1

CHOOSE TO BE HAPPY

Happy is the man who finds wisdom.

Proverbs 3:13

Rejoice in the Lord always.

Philippians 4:4

HAPPINESS in life is a choice. Not everything that happens to you will be good; bad things happen to good people. You might break a bone or wreck your car. You may lose your wallet or lose a lot of money in a financial deal, and the loss is beyond your control. And yes, there will be hurt; and yes, you will weep. But inwardly you can rejoice that you know God and that you are heading to be with God when you die. Happiness is not tied to a smiling face or physical response to circumstances. No! Happiness is tied to your relationship with God—your sins are forgiven, you belong to God, and He has a plan for your life (see Jeremiah 29:11). Remember, we don't rejoice in circumstances or in events, not even in victories; we are challenged to "rejoice in the Lord, always" (Philippians 4:4).

Lord, thank You for saving me, and sending Your Son, Jesus Christ, to live within my heart. You will guide me and You

---

have a plan for my life. I want to know Your will and pur-
pose for my life. Help me find it and follow it. Amen.

The Lord has promised to give you a rejoicing life, but you must want it, receive it by faith, and act on it. There is a big difference between inward joy and outward happiness. They feed on each other as you respond. Your inward happiness will influence your outward rejoicing. Therefore, always let the inward joy of the Lord shine forth.

Lord, I cannot always look within to find joy. I will look to
You and keep open my relationship with You. Give me Your
joy so I can rejoice on Earth and spread Your joy to others.
Amen.

READ:

Philippians 4:1-23

Day 2

CHOOSING GOD FIRST

But seek first the kingdom of God
and His righteousness, and all these
things shall be added to you.

Matthew 6:33

WHEN your first choice is God, it influences all the rest of your choices. Because when you put God first, you will want to honor and please Him with all your other choices. That means you will choose against evil activities, including evil entertainment, drink, and anything that is called *sinful pleasures*. When you choose God, you put Him first the way you do your special time and money. Choosing God first does not mean going to church all the time and always reading your Bible and praying. Not at all. It means doing all the necessary tasks and requirements you must do, but you do everything with His presence in your life, with His attitude, and you do it joyfully.

> *Lord, I have chosen You to live in my heart and guide my life. Shine Your love and grace through my actions and attitudes. May people see Jesus living in me. Use me for Your glory and purpose. Amen.*

The word "first" means Jesus has priority over/in your life. First means He is *number one*; so you think about Jesus first each day and continually all day, and you let Jesus control your life and thinking. So He is always present in your life. He will be *there* when you are not aware of His presence, but you can stop/pause to claim His presence/indwelling at any time. Jesus first means Jesus always, Jesus now.

> *Lord, I do that now. I submit my will to Your will. I give myself to You again, just as I did at salvation. I yield my past life and sins to You. Forgive me. I give my present life to You, and I yield my future to You. Amen.*

READ:

Matthew 6:19-34

Day 3

FINDING GOD'S PRESENCE

Not my will, but thine, be done.

Luke 22:42, KJV

JESUS is our example in everything, but especially in His attitude and practice of prayer. As Jesus approached the heavenly Father in prayer, He yielded His will to the direction of His heavenly Father. Have you made that commitment to always begin your prayers with yielding your will to God? God cannot answer your prayers if you ignore His will, or if you fight His will, or if you do the opposite of His will. If you want God's guidance/blessing on your life, you must be yielded to His will. Then you must actively search for His will and just as actively do His will.

> *Lord, I want Your blessing on all I am and all I do. Show me Your will. I will do it. When Your will is contrary to what I want, I will yield to You. When I have missed Your will because of ignorance, forgive me ... guide me to find Your will ... help me do Your will ... and bless me. Amen.*

Jesus was the only One who did not need to yield His will to the heavenly Father. That is because they are one in nature/unity. But because

Jesus paused to yield His will to the Father, I will do the same thing. We know in our hearts that God controls our lives. We feel His presence and know He is with us, but still we must submit our desires to Him by an act of our will surrendering to His will.

Lord, I surrender now. I submit my will to Your will. I give myself to You again, just as I did in salvation. I yield my past life and sins to You. Forgive me. I give my present life to You, and I yield my future to You. Amen.

READ:

Matthew 26:30-56

Day 4

GETTING ADVICE

Plans go wrong for lack of advice.

Proverbs 15:22, NLT

In the multitude of counselors, there is safety.

Proverbs 11:24

I N this book on making choices, seeking advice is one of the best ways to make good choices. We don't always know all the details/circumstances involved in the choices we face, so others can help us see both sides to our options. Perhaps they can see the dangers or consequences that we face. Also, they may see or understand all the ramifications of the choices we face. So we should seek their opinion/advice as we think and pray about decisions. But sometimes we forget to ask for their help. But even then we should try to look at our decisions through the eyes of others/family/friends.

> *Lord, help me with the many decision I make in life. Help me seek the help/advice of others. Give them honesty to help me, and give me wisdom/humility to receive their advice. Help me live a good life to Your glory, so help me make good decisions to find that good life. Amen.*

We all have family and friends who love us and want the best for our lives. We should pray for them as we receive their prayers for us. Then after their concerns, we should enjoy and benefit from their experiences of love/advice. Life is tough, and it's hard to make it by yourself, so learn to faith-walk with others.

> *Lord, thank You for family and friends and all they have done for me. Help me listen to them and learn from them. It is hard to make it by myself, so help me learn from others. Amen.*

READ:

Proverbs 15:1-33

Day 5

GROWING PAINS ARE OUR TEACHER

My troubles turned out all for the best—they forced me to learn from your textbook.

Psalm 119:71, MSG

THE next time you get hurt and suffer pain, remember, don't complain, and don't yell immediately for relief. Ask God what He is teaching you through your pain. God may be telling you what to do, or what not to do. But then your pain may have nothing to do with your actions. Sometimes our suffering comes from unexpected sources. So the next time pain hits and you cannot find relief, ask, "What is God teaching me?" Sometimes pain is calling you to seek the presence of God. It could be a time to fellowship with God, or learn from God, or it could even be an invitation to pray and seek God for relief. Maybe God wants to send His message to you about this particular pain.

Lord, I am praying to You about my pain. I don't like it and I want relief. But teach me what I should learn from this pain. Show me how to react. I will be patient and wait for Your answer. Amen.

C. S. Lewis said, "God whispers to us in our pleasure, speaks to us in our conscience, but shouts to us in our pain." Sometimes God sends pain to get our attention, and at others times He makes the pain excessive to get our full attention. Do you have pain? Do you need to talk to God about it?

Lord, I come praying about my pain. Take it away in Your goodness. If not, teach me what I am supposed to learn. Then help me live with this pain, and help me find Your presence. I am waiting on You. Amen.

READ:

Psalm 119:65-80

Day 6

HARD CHOICES

What to choose, I know not.

Philippians 1:22, ELT

WHEN Paul said he did not know what choice to make, he was in a Roman prison, facing possible execution/death. He did not know if he would live or die. When he could not control his life and the future was uncertain, he proclaimed, "For me, to live is Christ, and to die is gain" (Philippians 1:21). As I read that verse when I was a teenager just saved, my commitment was "to live for Christ." Now as I write this devotional, I am 89 years old, and my response is "to die is gain." Where are you today? Are you staring at life in the future, or is death a possibility in the future?

> *Lord, I made a choice to receive Jesus and live for Him when I was young. Thank You for a good life, and I praise You for letting me serve You. Help me use all my days/years to serve You ... and praise You .. and glorify You. Amen.*

Life is choice, and what you do with/for Christ will determine the quality/influence of the rest of your life. When the apostle Paul faced hard choices, he knew who he was (a follower of Christ). He knew he would always serve Christ ("for me, to live is Christ"). He knew he could do much for Christ ("I can do all things through Christ"). Paul lived in Jesus, who lived in him (see Galatians 2:20).

> *Lord, there are many hard choices in life because we don't always know what to do. But I chose You to save me, and then I chose to let You guide me. Now, I choose to abide in You and let You abide in me (see John 15:5). Amen.*

READ:

Philippians 1:1-30;
John 15:1-8

Day 7

MAKING CHOICES

I call heaven and earth as witnesses today ... I have
set before you life and death ... therefore choose life.

Deuteronomy 30:19

MAKE choices in keeping with your core values. These values involve your life, your time, and your future—do all things for Christ, to please Christ, and live for Christ. Other values are family, friends, and a good testimony for Christ. Another set of values is your time, talents, and treasures (money and resources); again, yield them to Christ to be used for His glory. Another set of values is worship, growing spiritually, and ministering for Christ. Make sure these have their rightful place in your life and are done for Christ. Did you notice that all the values listed above center on Christ? Therefore, your core value in life is the Lord Jesus Christ.

> *Christ, I thank You for everything I am and have physically.*
> *I praise You for saving me ... indwelling me ... leading me ...*
> *using me ... and protecting me. I commit the rest of my life to*
> *You. I will center on pleasing You and serving You. Amen.*

The core value of your life is really who you are. You may work for money, but it is to be used to serve Christ. You have family and friends, but you want Christ to use those relationships for His purpose and glory. You have many other areas, facets of life, but put Christ there. Put the Lord Jesus Christ at the center of your life.

Lord Jesus, come live at the center of my life. Be the central controlling force of all I do. Fill me with Your presence and shine Your glory through me. Amen.

READ:

Deuteronomy 19:1-20

Day 8

TWO APPROACHES TO YOUR PROBLEMS

Choose today whom you will serve ... but as for me and my family we will serve the Lord.

Joshua 24:15

LIFE is made up of all types of choices—some big and some little. Then some choices are life-directing, others inconsequential. Also, some choices lead you to God's favor; other choices lead to evil. What is the biggest choice you have ever made? Would you do the same today? Why? What about your choices for God? What was the most important one? It should be when you chose Jesus to be your Savior from sin. Then have you chosen to follow Jesus as His disciple? You should tell Him you will follow Him (see Luke 9:23). How about future choices? Have you ever asked God to help you make good choice in the future about sin ... life ... choices according to His plan for your life? Now is a good time to do it.

> *Lord Jesus, thank You for saving me and coming into my life. I will follow You. Lead me ... guide me ... protect me ... and use me. I commit myself to be Your follower. Amen.*

There's another decision. Have you ever asked God to help you make future healthy decisions? That means you want God to guide you in all your decision-making in life from now on. When you choose to make all decisions according to the will of God, it is a life-altering choice. You have turned the control of your life over to God so He can guide you in all future choices.

> *Lord, I make that decision now: I will seek Your guidance in all of my decisions. I will read Your Word to find Your will. I will pray to ask for Your guidance. I will yield to let You work in my life. I want to be Your follower. I want You to use me. Amen.*

READ:

Joshua 24:1-28

Day 9

OPEN DOOR OF OPPORTUNITIES

*There is a wide-open door for a great work
here, although many oppose me.*

1 Corinthians 16:9, NLT

SOME choices in life are easy to make, especially when there is a wide-open door of opportunity to serve God. Perhaps you don't have to struggle with decision-making. When the door opens, you might pray, *When, Lord?* Or, *How, Lord?* Or, *Give me strength ... resources ... support!* But when God opens the door, it is His invitation for you to follow Him into the opportunity. As you enter, make sure you are yielded to follow Him. Then make sure all sins or disobedience in your life have been taken to the cross of Christ for forgiveness. When you face God's door of opportunity, you will enter it with the indwelling of Jesus and His guidance.

> *Lord, give me eyes to see my doors of opportunity and give me wisdom to respond obediently. Help me walk into opportunity to serve You; while there, use me to minister for You. Amen.*

Not all doors in life are good, and not all doors are positive. Be careful of doors of entertainment and pleasures and activities. Make sure it is God's door. Remember, satan will have doors of sexual enticement, illegal money, and illicit days. Ask for God's wisdom as you approach all doors; make sure you know which door is God's opportunity.

Lord, give me spiritual eyes to see into Your doors of opportunity, and let those spiritual eyes take me away from wrong doors of disappointment and disaster. Keep me ... protect me ... and guide me into Your presence. Amen.

READ:

1 Corinthians 16:1-13

Day 10

COMMON-SENSE
DECISIONS

*We can make our plans, but the
Lord determines our steps.*

Proverbs 16:9, NLT

GOD gave us brains to guide our lives. Therefore, we are to learn as much as we can so God can best guide us according to facts/ data. Our minds should be well informed so they can guide our lives to be profitable servants for God. When it comes to decision-making, those who make the best decision can be used productively for God—when they make a decision according to God's plan and will. Sometimes we will make wrong decisions out of ignorance, but pray that God will help you decide properly and that He will always guide and protect you. Our verse today tells us to "make our plans" because "the Lord determines our steps." That is a great promise to claim as we go through life making life's decisions.

> *Lord, I yield my decision-making to You. Help me make Your decisions—right decisions—that will guide me rightly. Keep me from making wrong decisions; and when I do, forgive me ... guide me ... protect me ... help me. Amen.*

God tells us to make our plans, and we do that by searching for His plan for our lives and following it. Do you know God has a plan for your life (see Jeremiah 29:11, NLT)? God's plans are good, so when your decision is God's plan, it is a good decision. You have a heavenly Father who loves you and wants the best for your life. You can find that life when you are in a talking relationship with Him.

Father, I want to know Your plan for my life; show it to me. I will follow it and obey You. I will serve You and live for You. Use me to glorify You and Your kingdom. Amen.

READ:

Proverbs 16:1-33

Day 11

SOVEREIGN
GUIDANCE

And we know that all things work together
for good to those who love God, to those
who are the called according to His purpose
... conformed to the image of His Son.

Romans 8:28-29

WHEN problems frustrate you and it seems you don't know what to do, remember that God is overseeing your life. He is never caught off guard, and He never panics. Behind the scenes God is working out all things for the good of those whom He has called. To say God allows pressures and failures does not mean God planned for our failures or He caused our problems. No! But God is working behind the scenes to conform us to be like Jesus. So God uses "hard things" to make us stronger, and at the same time God uses our failures to make us tender and humble.

Lord, thank You for guiding my life. I want to be like Your Son, Jesus. Use every failure to make me stronger and use every success to make me better. At the end I will pray, "not I but Christ." Amen.

The word "predestinate" scares some people. Some think it means God controls our life like a little girl playing with her dolls. God knows everything we say, do, think, and how we respond. Others believe the opposite, that we are responsible for all and God is only an innocent by-stander watching everything we do. Both extremes are wrong. You are completely responsible for all you think and do and feel, yet God works it all out according to His plan for His glory.

Lord, I don't understand the word "predestinate." So I will think of You as best I can and as often as I can. Then I will do as much for You as often as I can, as best I can. Then I will ask for forgiveness and cleansing. Finally, I will worship You for Your powerful omnipotence. Amen.

READ:

Romans 8:1-39

Day 12

ASK FOR ANYTHING

And whatever you ask in My name, that I will
do, that the Father may be glorified in the Son.
If you ask anything in My name, I will do it.

John 14:13-14

JESUS told us to pray "asking" for "whatsoever." It looks like we can make successful decisions by prayer, or we can solve problems by asking God to solve them. At this place Jesus promises "whatsoever we ask," but at other places there are conditions for getting our prayers answered. We must confess our sins to be in fellowship with God (see 1 John 1:7-10). We must continue in prayer and fellowship with God (see Matthew 7:7). We must not ask for things motivated by lust or sin, or be sin controlled (see James 4:1-3). We must abide in Jesus to get our prayers answered (see John 15:7). Then we must ask for things in God's will, i.e., things He wants to give us (see 1 John 5:14).

Lord, I love fellowshipping with You, and I love to talk with
You in prayer. Teach me how to ask for things in prayer and
remind me when I ask in the wrong way, or for the wrong
things, or with the wrong attitude. Amen.

Remember, prayer is a two-way conversation. You must come open-hearted to God, and He must open His heart to you. That relationship must begin with honesty, truthfulness, and sincerity. So watch out for any wrong thing you request, and don't come to God with wrong attitudes. Above all, come believing God exists and that He rewards "those who sincerely seek Him" (Hebrews 11:6).

> *Lord, I will bring my problems to You for solutions, and in the same way I will pray about all my decisions. Help me solve my problems and give me strength to live victoriously for You. Teach me effective prayer and help me pray sincerely. Amen.*

READ:

1 John 5:1-21

Day 13

LISTEN BEFORE ANYTHING ELSE

Be still and know that I am God.

Psalm 46:10

THE first step in problem-solving is to stop before you start solving your problem—to listen. Why are you listening? To clear your mind and focus on your problem. Who are you listening for? God! And why are you listening for God? Because God knows all things, and He specifically knows three things about your problems. First, He knows what caused the problem. Don't you know that a "full knowledge about the problem is a half-solved problem?" Second, God knows what is needed to solve your problem. God knows the people involved ... the ingredients needed ... what you must do ... how to do it ... and when.

Lord, forgive me for trying to solve all my problems by myself. I yield my actions to You. I will do what You tell me to do. And, Lord, I will need Your help as I get into solving this problem. Show me what to do, how to do it, and when. Amen.

Third, God knows you; He knows your experience in solving problems. Plus, He knows your methods and how you go about solving problems. So listen to God; let Him show you things about yourself. When you know yourself, and you know how you approach problems, you are ready to get started.

> *Lord, I am listening to You, and I know You are God. Show me myself because You know me better than anyone. Show me what to do, then lead me as I solve my problems. And help me stay out of problems in the future. Amen.*

READ:

Psalm 42:1-11

Day 14

LET GOD SEARCH YOU

I, the Lord, search the heart, I test the mind,
even to give every man according to his
ways, according to the fruit of his doings.

Jeremiah 17:10

BEFORE you begin to search for answers to any problem facing you, or you struggle with decisions, stop all internal efforts. As you search for solutions or answers, realize that God is also searching, but He is not looking for ways to answer the questions you face. No! God know all things. But He is searching your heart. What is He looking for? God wants to know your fears, because He can help you through them. God wants to know your blind spots, the things you don't see and the answers you have not thought about. Also, God wants to know your motives and what you will do with the solution to your problem—when you find it, God wants to know what you will do after the problem is solved.

> *Lord, when You search my heart, You will find selfish mo-*
> *tivations and sin. Forgive me. You will find fear and igno-*
> *rance. Teach me. You will find wrong answers. Correct me.*
> *You will find emptiness. Fill me with Yourself, and Your*
> *peace, and Your guidance. Amen.*

For what is God searching? He is searching for truthfulness. Will you honestly face your problems? If you say yes, He will help you. Will you seek His help? If so, He will guide you. Will He find you confessing your sins and asking for cleansing? If so, He will forgive your sins, and cleanse your heart, and give you a new start in life, and He will help solve your problems.

> *Lord, I search for You because You are searching my heart. First Your cleansing in my heart, and Your peace in my mind. Then I will look forward to solving my problems and getting answers for decisions facing me. Amen.*

READ:

Jeremiah 17:5-18

Day 15

DON'T LET SIN INFLUENCE YOUR CHOICES

*Do not love the world or the things in the world.
If anyone loves the world, the love of the Father
is not in him. For all that is in the world—the
lust of the flesh, the lust of the eyes, and the pride
of life—is not of the Father but is of the world.*

1 John 2:15-16

WHEN facing choices, remember that you have a responsibility to make right choices—you owe it to God and yourself. But remember, you have a sinful heart that will deceive your thinking about things—especially spiritual matters. Today's verse warns you against three inward pressures. First, the "lust of the flesh" is the illegal cravings of the body. These are not the legitimate desires of food, water, air, etc. No, these desires fight against God and His principles of a pure/holy life. Don't give into things like alcohol, illicit sex, and drugs. Second, "the lust of your eyes" involves seeing and wanting and trying to get things you should not have. That could be cars, clothes, jewelry, and stuff you don't possess.

Lord, show me the lusts of my heart—sinful desires I did not know I had. Forgive me of my sinful lusts and give me spiritual eyes to see You and a desire for things You want me to have. Make me willing and happy to live with the things and stuff You give me. Amen.

The third force in your sinful heart is pride—putting yourself first, even above God. That does not mean we cannot have self-respect and proper self-motivations. No, we desire to be more than we can be. Sinful pride is living and working for sinful positions, and popularity we don't deserve, and positions we should not have. Pride is at the bottom of many sinful urges and actions.

Lord, forgive my selfish pride. I know I am egotistical, and I want power and control over people. Forgive me. Give me a clean heart to know You better and a clean life to serve You better. Amen.

READ:

1 John 2:1-27

Day 16

BAD CHOICES
FOR YOU

You must not covet your neighbor's house.
You must not covet your neighbor's wife,
male or female servant, ox or donkey, or
anything else that belongs to your neighbor.

Exodus 20:17, NLT

I N this study of good and bad choices, look within yourself to see if you have a problem with coveting. The tenth Commandment says, "Thou shalt not covet." Actually, "covet" comes from the old term "covert," i.e., a hiding place. When you covet something, you wrongly hide it in your heart. Today's coveting deals with "wishing enviously" for something, or "to desire illicitly." Technically your desires are wrong to want it. But more than desires, the thing may be wrong for you. So, before you go through the motion of a decision about something, perhaps the object you desire is wrong for anyone, and in this case, especially wrong for you. So, as you face a choice, step back to look within; look at your heart.

Lord, I have many choices in life; help me make them all for
You. As I look within my heart, I see a conflict between self
and spiritual choices. Forgive my sin and selfishness. Help

me know myself as You know me. Help me know myself honestly. Amen.

We all have desires because that is our human nature. When making choices, ask the following question: Will I break any of the Ten Commandments? Then ask, will I sin against God? Next ask, will God bless me with my answer/choices? Another question is, is this choice true to my Christian nature, and will it help me be a better person? Finally, ask, can I do this for God's glory and serve Him as I make this choice?

Lord, guide me as I make choices. I don't pray about all choices, so speak to me through Scripture and then through my conscience. Finally, help my family and friends guide me into right choices. Amen.

READ:

Exodus 20:1-26

Day 17

BAD CHOICES
LEAD TO DEATH

It is true! I have sinned against the Lord, the
God of Israel. Among the plunder I saw a
beautiful robe from Babylon, 200 silver coins,
and a bar of gold weighing more than a pound.
I wanted them so much that I took them.

Joshua 7:20-21, NLT

ACHAN was an obedient Jewish soldier who followed Joshua into the battle of Jericho. In the middle of the conflict, he saw/lusted after treasure—stole it—hid it under the rug in his tent (see Joshua 6:1-21). Israel lost the next battle, and God told them that "the children of Israel committed a trespass" (Joshua 7:1, KJV). God told Israel, "Do not take anything set apart for destruction ... silver, gold ... must be brought into the Lord's temple" (Joshua 6:18,20). Achan not only stole (broke the sixth Commandment), but he also took what was God's. As a result, he was punished and executed. His problem was not the items he stole; it was Achan's sinful heart.

Lord, help me learn from Achan's mistake and punishment.
Help me be honest in everything. But, Lord, it is not my
fingers that take things; it is my sinful heart that wrongly

---

desires things. Change my heart to obey You. Forgive and cleanse my heart. Amen.

Achan committed a sin in the heat of battle. Probably no one saw him or reported him. Maybe no one thought anything about it. But God saw, and God remembers all things. When Achan's sin came to public light, he was executed. God, who saw Achan, sees you and knows all you do—both big and small deeds. Ask God to give you clean fingers not to take things and a clean heart not to lust after things.

Lord, I come pleading the blood of Christ to cleanse my sins. Then I ask for the Holy Spirit to keep my heart from desiring things I should not have. Lead me to live an honest life. Amen.

READ:

Joshua 7:1-26

Day 18

PROBLEMS HELP YOU SERVE GOD BETTER

*But as for you, you meant evil against me; but
God meant it for good, in order to bring it about
as it is this day, to save many people alive.*

Genesis 50:20

IF ever there was a servant of God who went through troubles and suffering before fully being used of God, it was Joseph. Remember, Joseph was hated by his brothers, thrown in a pit, sold as a slave in Potiphar's house, where Potiphar's wife lied about Joseph, and was thrown into prison. How much more trouble could one person have? Yet God used Joseph's troubles and sufferings to make him wise, gracious, and powerful. When Joseph spoke, he voiced the authority of God. Just as Joseph's problems prepared him to serve God, so God has allowed problems in your life to prepare you to serve Him better.

Lord, help me learn from my troubles and sufferings. I don't like pain, and the lessons I learn are hard, yet I know You have a plan for my life (see Jeremiah 29:11). Help me find that plan and then guide me to be used according to my usability. Amen.

Troubles will make you more useful in God's plan for your life, so learn them quickly, and apply them thoroughly. Did you see the word you just used to pray to God—"usability"? God can only use you according to your usability. Perhaps more pain and greater suffering and emotional trouble will make you a greater servant for God. But if you learn these lessons of pain ... more thoroughly ... better, God can use you in a great way.

> *Lord, I want to learn; help me apply my mind, body, and soul to learn what You are teaching me. Help me to learn quickly and thoroughly, then use me in Your ministry. Amen.*

READ:

Hebrews 11:22;

Genesis 50:1-26

Day 19

MONEY CHOICES VERSUS LIFE CHOICES

What shall I do that I may inherit eternal life? ...
Go your way, sell whatever you have and give to the
poor ... and come, take up the cross, and follow Me.

Mark 10:17,21

THE rich young ruler came to follow Jesus, but Jesus told him to keep the commandments: don't steal, lie, murder, and hunger for more money. The young man replied, "All these thing I have kept since my youth" (Mark 10:20). When Jesus told him to sell everything, he went away sad, for he was very rich. So here is the question about money: Does your money own you, or do you own your money? Money is not wrong; so what is wrong? To lust for it ... lie to get it ... get it wrongly ... or to love it more than you love God. Yes, you need money to live, but work for it honestly, then make sure you live for God.

Lord, I have yielded my life and body to You; use me in Your
service. Now I yield my possessions and money to You; show
me how to use them for necessities, for life, and how much to
give to You. Amen.

After you give your life and possessions to God, the Bible suggests 10 percent shall be given to God for His work and church on Earth (see Malachi 3:10). You may give more to Him, but make sure to be financially responsible. Begin by dedicating all of your money to God, then ask how much to keep for necessities and how much to give to God's work.

Lord, I have given my soul, body, and life to You. I also have given You all of my worldly possessions and money. Guide me to spend it rightly on church tithes, necessities, etc. I am Yours, and I give all my money and possessions to You. Guide me in all areas of my life. Amen.

READ:

Mark 10:17-45

Day 20

A BAD CHOICE

*For Demas has forsaken me, having loved this
present world, and has departed for Thessalonica.*

2 Timothy 4:10

THIS section is about faith-walking through good choices and
bad ones. Demas was a disciple who helped Paul in ministry but
made a poor choice. When Paul wrote to Timothy from prison
in Rome, he asked the young disciple to come quickly, also, to bring his
cloak, books, parchments (see 2 Timothy 4:13). Demas could no longer
do all the needed tasks for Paul because he had left. The phrase "having loved this present world ... departed" suggests his wrong motives.
Demas was attracted by "this present world," not the call of Christ. We
can almost feel the loss as we read Paul's words telling Timothy that
Demas was gone.

> *Lord, there will always be worldly attractions to pull us away
> from following Jesus. I will "run the race ... looking unto Je-
> sus" (Hebrews 10:1-2). I will keep my eyes on my Savior so
> that I won't be tempted to leave His work. Amen.*

We don't know the internal pressure Demas faced. Was it physical
pressure, so he quit following Jesus? Was it financial pressure? Or was it
family problems? Again, we don't know. Were there issues of the lust of

the flesh ... lust of the eyes ... or pride of life? There are many attractions from the devil to draw us away from following Christ. But there is one thing that keeps us faithful—it is the Person of Christ.

Lord, I follow You because You have saved me and washed away my sins. You have given me new life—Your life—and Jesus lives in me. I will follow You because that is the most important decision in life. Amen.

READ:

2 Timothy 4:1-22

Day 21

WHEN IS A CHOICE GOOD?

*And she said, "Look, your sister-in-law has gone
back to her people and to her gods; return after your
sister-in-law." But Ruth said: "Entreat me not to
leave you, or to turn back from following after you;
for wherever you go, I will go; and wherever you
lodge, I will lodge; your people shall be my people,
and your God, my God. Where you die, I will die,
and there will I be buried. The Lord do so to me, and
more also, if anything but death parts you and me."*

Ruth 1:15-17

RUTH faced the choice of a lifetime. Her mother-in-law was heading back to Bethlehem to be with God's people in God's land.
Ruth's husband was dead, so was her father-in-law. She knew
no one in Bethlehem, or any of God's people in Judah. She would be
a foreigner with a foreign dialect and foreign clothes. But Ruth chose
rightly: "your God shall be my God" (v. 16). What a dramatic choice.
She did not know how she would earn a living, nor did she know where
she would sleep. But Ruth chose God, His people, His land, and His
salvation.

Lord, help me make good decisions as Ruth made a life-changing decision. I choose You and salvation. I choose godliness and to live Your life. I choose Your people, Your church, and service for You. I will follow Jesus. Amen.

When Ruth made her life-changing decision, it involved a new family, new in-laws, and a new way of living. Ruth did not know that God the Father would honor her difficult decision. She had no confidence about the future. So we see Ruth choosing to go to Bethlehem. God honored her choice and she became the grandmother of King David and was also in the line of the Messiah. Have you thought about your decisions? How the choices you make today—or soon—will influence your future, your children, God's work in the world?

Lord, I choose to follow You. I will not look back, and I will keep my eyes on You. I will trust You today, and I commit my future to You—as well as the future of my children and grandchildren. Amen.

READ:

Ruth 1:1-22

Day 22

MAKING DIFFICULT DECISIONS

*I call heaven and earth as witnesses today ... I have
set before you life and death ... therefore choose life.*

Deuteronomy 30:19

BEFORE making some difficult choices in life, we must first know ourselves and understand what we must do when making a *difficult* choice. First, you must make an internal commitment to *truth* and *honesty,* by determining to always chose *right*. When we are committed to God's standards of right and wrong, we begin to examine the facts/data involved in the decisions we face. When you are committed to God and truth, you are committed to being an honest person. And what does an honest person do? They honestly examine the facts/data and make an honest decision as they honestly face the facts.

> *Lord, help me always be honest with You, and with the Word
> of God, and with my conscience. Then give me strength to
> choose honestly in all the decisions of life. I want to please
> and honor You. Amen.*

When Moses knew he was leading God's people, he challenged them to make honest decisions and choose life by following God and His way.

That is the same challenge facing God's people today. We must honestly read and know the Scriptures so that we can make honest decisions to glorify Him. Then our decisions will be *best* for us.

Lord, I look to You in prayer when making decisions. But I always rely on the Word of God to guide me to know Your will in all decisions. Give me wisdom and courage to always choose right. Amen.

READ:

Deuteronomy 30:11-31

Day 23

BEFORE MAKING A DECISION

*"For I know the plans I have for you," declares
the Lord, "plans to prosper you and not to harm
you, plans to give you hope and a future."*

Jeremiah 29:11, NIV

BEFORE you make choices in life—both small and large decisions—always be aware that God has a plan for your life. Does God's will for you involve any large choices, or does it involve little ones? Let's back up to see God's overall plan. His will for all of His people is found in Scripture. So search the Bible to find God's desires for all; then fit yourself into God's overall plans for them and you. Next, search God's Word for His principles to guide your life. These involve guidance for both small and large decisions. How does God do that? He includes the eternal principles in His Word and allows us to apply them to our lives.

*Lord, I will seek Your will in all decisions. I yield myself to
know Your will and to study Scripture to find it. Then I will
apply Your will to my life. Give me self-discipline to do it,
and then give me wisdom to follow Your truth. Finally, give
me courage to obey as I apply Your will to my life. Amen.*

Since God has a plan for your life, do you know how to find it? If you do, have you searched for it this week—today? Will you do it the next time you read your Bible? But the important question is, will you do what God tells you to do? You see, God speaks to you for a purpose—so that you will obey His Word and follow His guidance. And as you do God's will, ask Him to help you do it.

Lord, I will study Your Word to find Your will. Then I will pray to understand it and then ask God to give me wisdom and courage to obey Your Word. Lord, speak. I wait for Your guidance. Amen.

READ:

Jeremiah 29:1-13

Day 24

CHOICES CONTROL YOUR LIFE

So, he [Paul], trembling and astonished,
said, "Lord, what do You want me to do?"

Acts 9:6

YOU must realize the best way to have a happy, prosperous life is to control your choices. Bad choices lead to bad results, and evil choices lead to evil. But spiritual choices led to spirituality. Paul was confronted with a vision of Jesus on the road to Damascus and yielded his life to the Lord. It was his first choice in the presence of God, and it was a life-transforming choice. Have you confronted Jesus in your prayers or Bible reading? Did you yield the control of your life to Him? Letting Jesus control your life—and your choices—is the first step to a profitable life, one filled with inner happiness and usefulness.

Lord, I do it now; I yield my life to You. And I will give You control over my choices. Give me wisdom to understand Your Word and help me find Your will for my life in Scripture. Amen.

All of our choices in life either make us or break us. So begin the road to success by yielding all your choices to Jesus. Let Him guide you to understand good choices and then give you wisdom and courage to make good choices. After all, a good life comes out of good choices.

Lord, I will study and learn Your Word to understand Your will for my life. Give me wisdom to make good choices, and then give me courage to choose what I know is good—for Your kingdom and for my life. Amen.

READ:

Acts 9:1-31

Day 25

CHOICE PROCESS

*This Book of the Law shall not depart from your
mouth, but you shall meditate in it day and night,
that you may observe to do according to all that
is written in it. For then you will make your way
prosperous, and then you will have good success.*

Joshua 1:8

YOU can successfully face the decisions of life—both small and
great—when you let the Word of God control your thinking
and your choice process. God put Joshua as leader of His people
and gave him the task of entering and conquering the Promised Land.
God reminded Joshua that success comes from commitment to what He
says—in Scripture, meditating on its words and obeying its commands.
God's challenge to Joshua applies to you today. If you will commit yourself to the God of the Bible, then obey His words and trust Him for
victory, you can make good decisions, i.e., win your daily battles.

> *Lord, I love Your Word. I will read it, memorize it, and
> meditate on its truth, and then live by its directions. Help
> me to apply Your Word to the decisions I make each day. I
> will live as close to the Scriptures as I can. Amen.*

When you remember the military battle Joshua won, also think about your spiritual battles that involve your daily choices. You can have victory as did Joshua when you are grounded in God's Word, and you can trust Him to guide you in the decisions you make daily. Look at the conditions, study the Bible, meditate on it, and obey it, "then your way will prosper, and you will be successful" (v. 8, ELT).

Lord, give me a desire to know Your Word, and then give me understanding as I meditate on Your Word. Finally, give me strength to obey Your Word and apply it to my life. Amen.

READ:

Joshua 1:1-9

Day 26

BETTER CHOICES

It is better to choose wisdom than gold, and
understanding is a better choice than silver.

Proverbs 16:16, ELT

YOU have many choices to make in life, but before you begin to consider both sides of a choice, there is a foundation that will help you. Proverbs directs us to first choose God's wisdom and understanding. When you choose God's wisdom, you have decided to give Him control of your life. You yield all future decision-making to God. What does that mean? First, when making a decision, you will think about God's plan/will for your life. Second, you will let God's principles for living guide your choices. Third, you will pray for His guidance in all decisions.

Lord, I yield my decision-making to You. I will seek to know
Your plan for my life and I will make choices in keeping with
Your design for my life. Give me strength and courage to keep
this commitment. Amen.

The next step in decision-making after yielding is to pray for understanding to know God's will and then commitment to doing what He shows you. Finally, you need courage to keep your commitment because many times circumstance fight your God choices. Because you have asked God to help you, you will need courage to carry out your commitment.

Lord, help me with my decision-making to always choose right and always follow through with my choices. Help me keep Your Word in my decision-making process. Amen.

READ:

Proverbs 16:1-33

Day 27

SINGING WHEN FACING DECISIONS

Let the message about Christ, in all its richness,
fill your lives. Teach and counsel each other with
all the wisdom he gives. Sing psalms and hymns
and spiritual songs to God with thankful hearts.

Colossians 3:16, NLT

YOU can confidently face decisions when you are being guided by the message of Christ, especially when it guides your thinking and decision-making process. You do that by letting its message control your life in all you do—more than just when you are making decisions. Today's passage refers to "singing psalms and hymns and spiritual songs" to God. The joy and happiness we experience as a result of the indwelling Word of God will then influence our attitude when facing problems. This means being influenced by "the spirit of the melody" as well as the message of the words.

Lord, I will learn and memorize Your Word so I can sing
its message. May the words/message give me direction as I
face decisions, and may the melody lift my spirit and expec-
tations. Amen.

God gives us His Word for many reasons. First, the content of the message saves us, and then the promise of the Word gives us strength and assurance. Next, the power of the indwelling Christ in the Word gives us victory over evil. Also, practical principles of daily living guide us in Christian living, testimony, and ministry.

Lord, thank You for the written message of Jesus Christ. I will read about Him and learn about His death and resurrection that saved me. I will live by the power of Your Word that helps me live victoriously over evil. Amen.

READ:

Colossians 3:1-25

Day 28

A DECISION THAT CHANGED THE WORLD

But Ruth said: "Entreat me not to leave you,
or to turn back from following after you; for
wherever you go, I will go; and wherever
you lodge, I will lodge; your people shall be
my people, and your God, my God."

Ruth 1:16

THIS was one of the greatest decisions to change a person's life. Ruth made a decision that changed her family and then her nation and history. Ruth, a Gentile girl, had married Chilion, a Jewish man, whose family had left God's Promised Land to live in the well-watered plains of Moab, a Gentile culture. But all the men in this Jewish family died. When the mother of the family decided to return to Bethlehem in the Holy Land, Ruth, the daughter-in-law, chose to go with her mother-in-law. It was about more than money and a family relationship—God was her primary motivation. When Ruth said, "[Y]our God shall be my God," it was her faith that guided her decision, and she went to the Holy Land without children, without any promise or hope of a future.

Lord, thank You for the example of Ruth, whose choice involved her whole life and future. I will make the same type of choice. I choose to follow You ... serve You ... and minister for You. Help me influence the world. Amen.

When Ruth left her Gentile home, there was no promise waiting for her in Bethlehem. Yet God saw her heart. She had married into the line that ultimately led to the coming Messiah. Think of it: through Ruth came Israel's Messiah—our Lord Jesus Christ. Could you make a small decision that could change your life forever? Or that could change your family, or your church, or your nation? Only God knows what happens when small decisions are made to glorify Him.

Lord, I want to make all my decisions so that I will honor You. Guide me to learn how to make decisions—and when to make them—and help me value my decision-making ability. Amen.

READ:

Ruth 1:1-22

Day 29

TAKE OWNERSHIP OF YOUR CHOICES

Receive God's instructions, rather than silver,
and choose knowledge rather than gold.

Proverbs 8:10, ELT

YOU have probably made several bad choices in life. Some of them were worse than others. However, they were your choices. You cannot blame others, or circumstances, or anything else. Because bad choices were your choice—own them ... take responsibility for them ... and learn from them. First ask God's forgiveness for all sins and bad choices (see 1 John 1:5-10). Then determine not to make that kind of bad choice again. Next, learn from them; learn positive lessons about how to not make that bad choice again, or even any choice that is like the one that hurt. Everyone makes bad choices—you do, I do, everyone does —so let's look to the future and plan to make good choices.

Lord, forgive me for my sins, or stupidity, or carelessness
that made me make a bad choice. Cleanse me and renew
my mind to learn from my choices. Guide me to make better
choices in the future. Amen.

Learning to make good choices begins by listening to your new nature that God gave you when you were born again (see 2 Corinthians 5:17). Second, learn/saturate your mind with Scriptures so you can think God's thoughts—but even better, so you can think like God and make choices as God would make. Then pray: pray daily about all decisions/choices, and then pray specifically for the choice that faces you now. The bigger and more serious the choice, the longer you pray—maybe even fast.

> *God, forgive me for all past bad decisions I have made. Help me learn from them; now help me overcome my consequences. Guide me in my present/future decisions to make them according to the teaching of Scripture and Your will. Amen.*

READ:

Proverbs 8:1-36

Day 30

TO PROTECT AGAINST OURSELVES

And lest I should be exalted above measure by the abundance of the revelations, a thorn in the flesh was given to me, a messenger of Satan to buffet me, lest I be exalted above measure.

2 Corinthians 12:7, NLT

PAUL was given a problem/illness that gave him constant pain. Why would God do that to His choice messenger? Why would God do that to one who served God with great fruit? Because pain keeps us from mistakes/more illness/death. Pain also keeps us from pride and selfish desires. In Paul's case, God gave Paul a pain so he would exalt Jesus Christ and not himself. Some think Paul didn't have a sinful nature and could do no wrong; they are wrong. Read Romans 7: "I want to do what is right, but I don't do it. Instead, I do what I hate" (v. 15, NLT). So God gave Paul a painful thorn in the flesh so he would exalt Jesus Christ, not himself.

Lord, help me think right ... plan right ... and do right so You don't have to give me a "thorn in the flesh." I want to serve You— and serve You without pain. But if You choose pain to help me serve You better, then, Lord, I submit myself to You. Amen.

God gives pain for many reasons—sometimes He allows it; other times He plans it. Whatever the reason, learn the lesson God has for you in pain. Perhaps if we learned our lessons quicker and better, we might not have pain. But that is not always the case. Sometimes God's best servants seem to have the most pain. Whatever God's reasons, "all things work together for good to those who love Him" (Romans 8:28).

Lord, I will try to learn as much as possible—as quickly as possible—to bypass pain. But if that is not possible, I yield myself to You. It is more important for You to be glorified than for me to bypass pain. Amen.

READ:

2 Corinthians 12:1–13:10

Day 31

FAITH-WALKING THROUGH PROBLEMS

As you have received Christ Jesus as your
Lord, continue to faith-walk in Him.

Colossians 2:6, ELT

SOMEONE said there will always be death and taxes, and we can add to that statement, *problems.* God provided a perfect world run by His immutable laws. But the introduction of sin introduced "thorns and thistles" growing among God's law of nature (see Genesis 3:16-19). These problems are obstacles in our lives, to our happiness and success as we grow through life. You must not only expect problems but also plan to face them, live through them, and solve them. You do this by *faith-walking* through problems. Remember, to faith-walk is a race, looking to Jesus (see Hebrews 12:1-2). Since you will have problems, who better to help you through them than Jesus.

> *Lord, forgive me for continually focusing on my problems.*
> *Sometimes they discourage me. Remind me to look to Jesus*
> *when problems come. I know He will help me through them,*
> *because He has done it in the past. Amen.*

Faith is simply *looking to Jesus*. So when problems arise, don't get discouraged; expect them. Don't face them alone; let Jesus help you. Don't give up; be faithful as Jesus went faithfully through the problems facing Him as He died on the cross for us. Remember, Jesus indwells you (see Galatians 2:20) and He will walk with you. Therefore, you can overcome problems and win with Jesus.

Lord, thank You for understanding my weaknesses. And thank You for forgiving my sin of complaining and giving up. But most of all, thank You for giving me strength to overcome obstacles and be victorious with Your help (see 2 Corinthians 2:14). Amen.

READ:

2 Corinthians 2:14-17;

1 Corinthians 15:51-58

Day 32

CHOOSE TO CONTROL YOUR INNER THOUGHTS

*We even fight to capture every thought until
it acknowledges the authority of Christ.*

2 Corinthians 10:5, Phillips

As we approach our outside problems—those we face in life—first we must control our inner thoughts. When we get our thinking under control, then we can focus on the outward problems we face. As a follower of Christ, you can get His help to control your thinking. You begin by yielding control of your mind to Christ. Next, you reject evil thoughts and anything that will lead you to sin. Third, you pray; ask the Lord to help you focus on the problem at hand. Then ask Him to help you understand your problem(s) and focus on the solution.

*Lord, I begin solving my problem(s) by asking You to clear
my mind and then help me focus on the problem at hand.
Guide me to various ways to solve my problems, and then
help me choose the best solution. Then help me solve it. Amen.*

Now that you have prayed, you are ready to apply the solution. You have looked at many answers, but you must choose the best solution. Ask God to give you insight. Next, pray to ask God to give you wisdom as you apply the best solution. Then ask God to use you and guide you as you walk by faith through the problem.

> *Lord, I want Your strength to reject wrong answers and unacceptable solutions to my problems. Guide my thinking and lead me to make right choices. Then help me as I go forward in life. Amen.*

READ:

2 Corinthians 10:1-18

Day 33

CHOOSE TO GIVE
YOUR BODY TO GOD

*I plead with you to give your bodies to
God ... a living and holy sacrifice.*

Romans 12:1, NLT

PAUL gave us both an exhortation and an example that we should
yield/give control of our bodies to God. Look at the two pur-
poses. First, your body should be a living sacrifice. That means
much more than presenting a living animal to be sacrificed according to
Old Testament law. No! It means God wants you alive, with full intel-
lect, emotions, and will. God wants every part of your physical, mental,
and spiritual life. He has a plan for how you should live. But second,
God wants a holy sacrifice. That means separation from sin—pure—
and committed to God. God wants followers with holy thinking, holy
desires, and holy actions. That means completely holy, from the outer
activities to inward thinking.

*Lord, I want Your help when I face problems today. So I
have yielded my life and body to You. Then I need Your inner
guidance. I yield my inner life to You. Forgive me of my sins,
cleanse me, fill me, and use me. Amen.*

Give yourself completely to God because He wants more than what/ who you are today. So yield your future to Him. God wants your inward self—the one that controls your thinking, feelings, and actions. Also, God wants your future self. God wants to control who you will be tomorrow, next week, and next year. God not only wants you, but He wants every part of you.

> *Lord, forgive me when I have held back and not yielded to You. Cleanse me and give me strength to face today ... tomorrow ... and beyond. I yield myself to You. Make me what You want me to be. Amen.*

READ:

Romans 12:1-21

Day 34

CHOICES YOU
DID NOT MAKE

He chose us in Him before the
foundation of the world.

Ephesians 1:4

The Lamb of God who takes away
the sins of the world.

John 1:29

THERE are choices that you did not make that have determined your future destination after death. You were chosen by God because He loves you and wants you to follow Him. He chose you before the earth was formed. How could that happen? Since there is no time with God, He lives above time. Time is the measurement between actions and events, so the eternal God is not controlled by time. He created time and now controls what happens in time. Therefore, at a time in eternity past, God loved you, chose you, and now He is working out that choice in time—the time when you are alive and living.

Lord, thank You for choosing me before I chose You. Thank You for loving me before I loved You. Thank You for putting me in the time where I am now living, and among my parents who gave me birth. Now I want to live for You. Amen.

"But when the fullness of the time had come, God sent forth His Son, to be born" (Galatians 4:4). So there was a time—God's time—when His Son was born and another time when His Son died to forgive your sins. These were God's chosen times. Then your time came to be born, and another time when you were saved. When you made a choice to accept Christ as Savior, your sins were forgiven and God gave you a new life—eternal life.

Lord, thank You for time. Thank You for that time when I asked You to forgive my sins—and You did. Thank You for that time when I asked Jesus to come into my heart—and He did. Amen.

READ:

Ephesians 1:1-14

Day 35

BECAUSE GOD CHOSE YOU

You have not chosen Me, but I have chosen you.

John 15:16

THE greatest choice in eternity was not when you chose Jesus to be saved. No! Before that—in eternity past—Jesus chose you to belong to Him. First, He knows us, and second, He chooses us—that is a *hallelujah moment*! Praise God we were chosen! But even greater is when Jesus left Heaven to come to Earth where He would die for our sins. And not only for our sins, but for the sins of everyone in our families—for the sins of the world (see John 3:16; 1 John 2:1-2). Christ's choice of you was eternity based, for it happened before the foundation of the world. But your choice of Christ is life-changing because He transformed you to be like Him (see 2 Corinthians 5:17).

Lord, thank You for choosing me before I was born, even before You created the first person. Thank You because Your choice gives me inner confidence that I will spend eternity with You. Amen.

So we humans think in terms of the minutes/hours on our watches. But God thinks bigger—He thinks eternity. His thinking and choosing are not limited by human time or human space. From eternity past, you were chosen to live with the Father in Heaven—for eternity.

Lord, forgive me for always thinking in terms of human limitation. Stretch my imagination to dream of eternal Heaven with You. Give me minute-by-minute confidence of Your eternal salvation. Amen.

READ:

Ephesians 1:1-14

PART THREE

FAITH
WALKING
through
PROBLEMS

LESSONS

Lesson 1:

ANSWER KEY

APPROACHING PROBLEMS IN YOUR LIFE

A. ATTITUDES TOWARD PROBLEMS

As you have received Christ Jesus as your Lord, continue to faith-walk in Him. (Colossians 2:6, ELT)

1. The "Towns frustration" with problems. Why **me**? Why **now**? Why **this**?

2. Wrong attitudes about problems:

    a. You are **unsaved**.

    b. You are **unspiritual**.

    c. God has **forsaken** you.

3. Health problems—solving attitudes:

    a. You can't **run from** them.

    b. You can't keep problems **from happening**.

    c. You can **solve** them.

---

4. Causes of problems:

    a. **Change**. "Any change for any reason for any purpose is deplorable" (Duke of Canterbury).

    b. **Differences**. Usually different ethnic backgrounds, experiences, child rearing, age, expectations, etc.

    c. **Circumstances**. Personal needs, space, money, tools, skills, etc.

5. Three questions to ask:

    a. How big is the problem? It might be smaller; a well-defined problem is a half-solved problem. Need **objective eyes**.

    b. Who is involved in the problem? Most problems are a **conflict of attitudes**.

    c. What does the larger group think about the problem? When you ask for opinions, you get people's support/help.

6. Three wrong attitudes toward problems:

    a. **Fuss**—preach against it.

    b. **Fight**—organize resistance.

    c. **Die**—either you kill it or it kills you.

7. Three problem-solving eyes:

    a. Eyes to see the positive. "Lord, increase our faith" (Luke 17:5).

    b. Eyes to see **people involved**.

    c. Eyes to see beyond **failure**. "Looking unto Jesus" (Hebrews 12:2).

B. STEP-BY-STEP PROBLEM-SOLVING

1. Get the <u>facts.</u>

    a. Gather—files, records, phone records, lists, etc.

    b. Define the problem (write out) before trying to solve.

        You make good decisions on good information.

        You make bad decisions on bad information.

2. Establish biblical principles.

    a. The Bible is our **<u>operator's manual</u>**.

    b. Search secular sources for **<u>their solutions</u>**.

3. Evaluate the facts.

    a. Find the cause of problem.

    b. Define the problem.

4. Determine various solutions to the problem.

    a. God does not speak through a vacuum but through **<u>information/facts</u>**.

    b. Making a list of solutions may help you see a **<u>solution</u>**.

5. Choose/apply the best solution.

    a. In life, no perfect conclusions, only **<u>best solutions</u>**.

    b. **<u>Yield</u>** problem to God.

    c. **<u>Ask</u>** what God is teaching you through this process.

C. PRACTICAL PRINCIPLES

1. The weightier your decision, the broader your information gathering, the longer the time spent in prayer, fasting, and considering the options. The more severely your problem shakes your equilibrium, spend **more time** and **more intensity** seeking your solution.

2. Plan Bible reading that deals with **problem-solving**, and devotional reading that focuses on **God and worship**. These times your solution will pop into your thinking.

3. Pray about every possible **decision** and about the possible **solutions**.

4. Write and rewrite your problem and **possible solutions**.

5. Write out all **possible solutions** before attempting to apply one.

6. In your darkest hour, remember that God has an answer/solution. "I being in the way, the Lord led me" (Genesis 24:27). You must be **in the way**.

Lesson 1:

QUESTIONS

APPROACHING PROBLEMS IN YOUR LIFE

A. ATTITUDES TOWARD PROBLEMS

As you have received Christ Jesus as your Lord, continue to faith-walk in Him. (Colossians 2:6, ELT)

7. The "Towns frustration" with problems. Why _____?
   Why _____? Why _____?

8. Wrong attitudes about problems:

   d. You are _____ .

   e. You are _____ .

   f. God has _____ you.

9. Health problems—solving attitudes:

   a. You can't _____ them.

   b. You can't keep problems _____ .

   c. You can _____ them.

10. Causes of problems:

    a. _____ . "Any change for any reason for any purpose is deplorable" (Duke of Canterbury).

    b. _____ . Usually different ethnic backgrounds, experiences, child rearing, age, expectations, etc.

    c. _____ . Personal needs, space, money, tools, skills, etc.

11. Three questions to ask:

    a. How big is the problem? It might be smaller; a well-defined problem is a half-solved problem. Need _____ .

    b. Who is involved in the problem? Most problems are a _____ .

    c. What does the larger group think about the problem? When you ask for opinions, you get people's support/help.

12. Three wrong attitudes toward problems:

    a. _____ —preach against it.

    b. _____ —organize resistance.

    c. _____ —either you kill it or it kills you.

13. Three problem-solving eyes:

    a. Eyes to see the positive. "Lord, increase our faith" (Luke 17:5).

    b. Eyes to see _____ .

    c. Eyes to see beyond _____ . "Looking unto Jesus" (Hebrews 12:2).

B. STEP-BY-STEP PROBLEM-SOLVING

1. Get the _____ .

    a. Gather—files, records, phone records, lists, etc.

    b. Define the problem (write out) before trying to solve.

        You make good decisions on good information.

        You make bad decisions on bad information.

2. Establish biblical principles.

    a. The Bible is our _____ .

    b. Search secular sources for _____ .

3. Evaluate the facts.

    a. Find the cause of problem.

    b. Define the problem.

4. Determine various solutions to the problem.

    a. God does not speak through a vacuum but through
        _____ .

    b. Making a list of solutions may help you see a _____ .

5. Choose/apply the best solution.

    a. In life, no perfect conclusions, only _____ .

    b. _____ problem to God.

    c. _____ what God is teaching you through this
        process.

C. PRACTICAL PRINCIPLES

1. The weightier your decision, the broader your information gathering, the longer the time spent in prayer, fasting, and considering the options. The more severely your problem shakes your equilibrium, spend_____ and _____ seeking your solution.

2. Plan Bible reading that deals with _____ , and devotional reading that focuses on _____ . These times your solution will pop into your thinking.

3. Pray about every possible _____ and about the possible _____ .

4. Write and rewrite your problem and _____ .

5. Write out all _____ before attempting to apply one.

6. In your darkest hour, remember that God has an answer/solution. "I being in the way, the Lord led me" (Genesis 24:27). You must be _____ .

Lesson 2:

ANSWER KEY

SUCCESSFUL PROBLEM-SOLVING

A. APPROACHING YOUR PROBLEMS

Now therefore, fear the Lord, serve Him in sincerity and in truth, and put away the gods which your fathers served on the other side of the River and in Egypt. Serve the Lord! And if it seems evil to you to serve the Lord, choose for yourselves this day whom you will serve, whether the gods which your fathers served that were on the other side of the River, or the gods of the Amorites, in whose land you dwell. But as for me and my house, we will serve the Lord. (Joshua 24:14-15)

1. Life is a **choice**. People have the most success when they make right choices—most of the **time**—about **important areas** at the **right time**.

2. God, who knows the dangers, gives negative warning.

   a. The Ten Commandments. Thou shalt not have any gods or idols, take God's name in vain, misuse the Sabbath, dishonor parents, murder, commit adultery, steal, lie, or covet things.

   b. Over 600 **negative** rules.

---

3. God spells out/directs through:

   a. Sovereign **guidance** (see Romans 8:28)

   b. Inwardly (see Romans 8:14)

   c. Opportunities/open doors (see 1 Corinthians 16:9)

   d. Our yielded spirits (see Romans 12:1-2)

   e. Our spiritual gifts (see 1 Corinthians 7:7)

   f. Our common sense (see Proverbs 16:9)

   g. Prayer (see Matthew 7:7)

   > The wrong decision at the wrong time—**disaster**

   > The wrong decision at the right time—**mistake**

   > The right decision at the wrong time—**unacceptable**

   > The right decision at the right time—**success**

B. 10 PRINCIPLES FOR MAKING SUCCESSFUL DECISIONS

1. Take time to **listen** to God's voice. "Be still and know that I am God" (Psalm 46:10).

2. Ask and answer questions about yourself. God comes with questions: "Adam, where are you?" (Genesis 3:9). "Cain, why are you angry?" (Genesis 4:6). Paul asked, "Who are you, Lord?" (Acts 9:5).

3. Recognize objective truth. Sometime God's voice is **loud**; other times it is "a still small voice." Sometimes God is **silent**. Yet, truth like gravity always stands there next to us. Two continuous problems: our **memory** and **insight**.

4. Stop all self-effort and yield to God. "Whatever you plan to do, put your whole life into it" (Colossians 3:23, ELT).

5. Pay attention to your physical. Sometimes your body speaks so loudly you cannot hear **yourself thinking**.

6. Pay attention to your spiritual:

   a. Yield like Paul. "Lord, what would You have me do?" (Acts 9:6).

   b. Search with your whole heart. "You will seek Me, and find Me, when you search ... your whole heart" (Jeremiah 29:13).

   c. Allow God to search/**ask you questions**. "I, the Lord, search the heart" (John 17:10).

   d. Let the Holy Spirit **show you**. "The Holy Spirit ... will teach you all things and bring all things to your remembrance" (John 14:26).

   e. **Study**. "Study to shew thyself approved unto God, a workman that needeth not to be ashamed, rightly dividing the word of truth" (2 Timothy 2:15, KJV).

   f. Searching prayer. "Search me O God" (Psalm 139:23).

7. Obey what you learn. "I was not disobedient" (Acts 26:19).

8. Be patient.

    a. God speaks <u>slowly</u>, like the dawning of a new day.

    b. <u>Sometimes suddenly</u>. Archimedes: "Eureka ... I found it."

9. Be open to insight from others. Ask. Paul prayed and God sent **Ananias**: "Brother Saul ... God sent me ... receive your sight" (Acts 9:17).

10. Be prepared to be misunderstood. God spoke to Paul on the Damascus Road, not to the others traveling with him.

    a. Did not see Jesus.

    b. Did not fast for answer.

    c. Ananias did not come to them.

Lesson 2:

SUCCESSFUL PROBLEM-SOLVING

A. APPROACHING YOUR PROBLEMS

Now therefore, fear the Lord, serve Him in sincerity and in truth, and put away the gods which your fathers served on the other side of the River and in Egypt. Serve the Lord! And if it seems evil to you to serve the Lord, choose for yourselves this day whom you will serve, whether the gods which your fathers served that were on the other side of the River, or the gods of the Amorites, in whose land you dwell. But as for me and my house, we will serve the Lord. (Joshua 24:14-15)

1. Life is a _____ . People have the most success when they make right choices—most of the _____ —about _____ at the _____ .

2. God, who knows the dangers, gives negative warning.

   a. The Ten Commandments. Thou shalt not have any gods or idols, take God's name in vain, misuse the Sabbath, dishonor parents, murder, commit adultery, steal, lie, or covet things.

   b. Over 600 _____ rules.

---

3. God spells out/directs through:

   a. Sovereign _____ (see Romans 8:28)

   b. Inwardly (see Romans 8:14)

   c. Opportunities/open doors (see 1 Corinthians 16:9)

   d. Our yielded spirits (see Romans 12:1-2)

   e. Our spiritual gifts (see 1 Corinthians 7:7)

   f. Our common sense (see Proverbs 16:9)

   g. Prayer (see Matthew 7:7)

   The wrong decision at the wrong time— _____

   The wrong decision at the right time— _____

   The right decision at the wrong time— _____

   The right decision at the right time— _____

B. 10 PRINCIPLES FOR MAKING SUCCESSFUL DECISIONS

1. Take time to _____ to God's voice. "Be still and know that I am God" (Psalm 46:10).

2. Ask and answer questions about yourself. God comes with questions: "Adam, where are you?" (Genesis 3:9). "Cain, why are you angry?" (Genesis 4:6). Paul asked, "Who are you, Lord?" (Acts 9:5).

3. Recognize objective truth. Sometime God's voice is _____ ; other times it is "a still small voice." Sometimes God is _____ . Yet, truth like gravity always stands there next to us. Two continuous problems: our _____ and _____ .

4. Stop all self-effort and yield to God. "Whatever you plan to do, put your whole life into it" (Colossians 3:23, ELT).

5. Pay attention to your physical. Sometimes your body speaks so loudly you cannot hear _____ .

6. Pay attention to your spiritual:

    a. Yield like Paul. "Lord, what would You have me do?" (Acts 9:6).

    b. Search with your whole heart. "You will seek Me, and find Me, when you search ... your whole heart" (Jeremiah 29:13).

    c. Allow God to search/ _____ . "I, the Lord, search the heart" (John 17:10).

    d. Let the Holy Spirit _____ . "The Holy Spirit ... will teach you all things and bring all things to your remembrance" (John 14:26).

    e. _____ . "Study to shew thyself approved unto God, a workman that needeth not to be ashamed, rightly dividing the word of truth" (2 Timothy 2:15, KJV).

    f. Searching prayer. "Search me O God" (Psalm 139:23).

7. Obey what you learn. "I was not disobedient" (Acts 26:19).

8. Be patient.

    a. God speaks _____ , like the dawning of a new day.

    b. _____ . Archimedes: "Eureka ... I found it."

9. Be open to insight from others. Ask. Paul prayed and God sent _____ : "Brother Saul ... God sent me ... receive your sight" (Acts 9:17).

10. Be prepared to be misunderstood. God spoke to Paul on the Damascus Road, not to the others traveling with him.

    a. Did not see Jesus.

    b. Did not fast for answer.

    c. Ananias did not come to them.

Lesson 3:

A STUDY OF GOOD AND BAD CHOICES

A. WHY PEOPLE MAKE POOR CHOICES

Don't ask me to leave you and go back to my old ways. Wherever you go, I will go. Wherever you live, I will live. Your people will be my people, and your God will be my God. Wherever you die, there I will be buried. (Ruth 1:16-17)

1. They **guess**—because they don't have enough information.

2. They choose—based on **bad information**.

    People make good choices on good information.

    They make bad choices on bad information.

    Without any information, they make **lucky choices**.

    Some have **good luck**; others have **bad luck**.

3. They never **learned how** to make decisions.

4. They developed a **pattern** of wrong decisions.

---

5. They follow their **heroes**, who made wrong decisions, i.e., Hitler, Jim Jones.

6. They listen to wrong **counselors**. "The advice of the wicked is treacherous" (Proverbs 12:5, NLT).

7. They are headed in the **wrong direction**.

    The wrong decision when going the wrong way—**disaster**

    The wrong decision when going the right way—**mistake**

    The right decision at the wrong time—**unacceptable**

    The right decision at the right time—**success**

8. They don't know their **self-limitations**. Some want to be president but can't pass college courses.

9. They don't know the **circumstances**. They enroll in a college that is going bankrupt (Wesley Sculpture)?

10. Some Christians are ignorant of their **spiritual gift**. "Each one has a proper gift of God" (1 Corinthians 7:7, ELT).

11. Some Christians don't know how to find the **will of God** for their lives, i.e., "The perfect will of God" (Romans 12:1).

12. In this lesson, a decision is a **one-time selection**, while choices mean a **series of bad options**.

B. WHAT INFLUENCE DOES SIN HAVE ON CHOICES?

Do not love the world or the things in the world. If anyone loves the world, the love of the Father is not in him. For all that is in the world—the lust of the flesh, the lust of the eyes, and the pride of life—is not of the Father but is of the world. (1 John 2:15-16)

1. The lust of the flesh is fulfilling bodily desires.

   a. This is not **basic bodily needs** God created in us, e.g., air, exercise, food, etc.

   b. This is **fleshly desires**, e.g., illicit sex, drug addictions, alcohol, gluttony, body worship with exercise, cosmetic surgery, etc.

2. The lust of the eyes wants things we see that we don't need or shouldn't have.

   a. This is not seeing things we **need** to live, serve God, and grow to maturity.

   b. This is lusting after things to fulfill an evil desire, e.g., money, stuff, things, gadgets, or **what our neighbor has**. "Thou shalt not covet thy neighbor's house" (Exodus 20:17).

3. The pride of life is exalting self beyond what is legal or what God wants for us.

   a. Pride is not self-respect, self-confidence, or self-acceptance, which we must have for a **healthy personality**.

   b. Pride is seeking to be something we are not and something we shouldn't be, e.g., **power**, position, **control of others**, glory, or exaltation.

C. PEOPLE WHO MADE BAD CHOICES

1. Lot chose the "well-watered plains" and lost **his family**.

2. Samson chose "sex" and lost his **life and reputation**.

3. Achan chose covetousness: "When I saw among the spoils a beautiful Babylonian garment, two hundred shekels of silver, and a wedge of gold weighing fifty shekels, I coveted them and took them" (Joshua 7:21). Achan was **stoned to death**.

4. The rich young ruler chose **things**. "He had great possessions" (Mark 10:22)

5. Demas chose a **worldly lifestyle**. "Demas hath forsaken me, having loved this present world" (2 Timothy 4:10, KJV).

D. PEOPLE WHO MADE GOOD CHOICES

1. Joshua. "Choose you this day whom you will serve ... but as for me and my house, we will serve the Lord" (Joshua 24:15).

   a. He had a lifetime of good choices.

   b. He was "faithful to death" (Revelation 2:10).

2. Ruth. "Thy God shall be my God" (Ruth 1:16).

   a. She chose when no one encouraged or supported her decision.

   b. She chose when there was **no other option**.

3. Esther. "If I perish, I perish" (Esther 4:16).

    a. She chose when there were no other options.

    b. She chose knowing she could **die for her choice**.

4. Solomon chose wisdom.

    At Gibeon the Lord appeared to Solomon in a dream by night; and God said, "Ask! What shall I give you?" "Therefore, give to Your servant an understanding heart to judge Your people, that I may discern between good and evil. For who is able to judge this great people of Yours?" The speech pleased the Lord, that Solomon had asked this thing. Then God said to him: "Because you have asked this thing, and have not asked long life for yourself, nor have asked riches for yourself, nor have asked the life of your enemies, but have asked for yourself understanding to discern justice, And I have also given you what you have not asked: both riches and honor, so that there shall not be anyone like you among the kings all your days." (1 Kings 3:5,9-12)

    a. We don't know what will happen to the things we **turn down**.

    b. The greatest choice is to be **wise**.

Lesson 3:

A STUDY OF GOOD AND BAD CHOICES

A. WHY PEOPLE MAKE POOR CHOICES

Don't ask me to leave you and go back to my old ways. Wherever you go, I will go. Wherever you live, I will live. Your people will be my people, and your God will be my God. Wherever you die, there I will be buried. (Ruth 1:16-17)

1. They _____ —because they don't have enough information.

2. They choose—based on _____ .

    People make good choices on good information.

    They make bad choices on bad information.

    Without any information, they make _____ .

Some have _____ ; others have _____ .

3. They never _____ to make decisions.

4. They developed a _____ of wrong decisions.

5. They follow their **heroes**, who made wrong decisions, i.e., Hitler, Jim Jones.

6. They listen to wrong _____ . "The advice of the wicked is treacherous" (Proverbs 12:5, NLT).

7. They are headed in the _____ .

   The wrong decision when going the wrong way—

   _____

   The wrong decision when going the right way—

   _____

   The right decision at the wrong time—

   _____

   The right decision at the right time—

   _____

8. They don't know their _____ . Some want to be president but can't pass college courses.

9. They don't know the _____ . They enroll in a college that is going bankrupt (Wesley Sculpture)?

10. Some Christians are ignorant of their _____ . "Each one has a proper gift of God" (1 Corinthians 7:7, ELT).

11. Some Christians don't know how to find the **will of God** for their lives, i.e., "The perfect will of God" (Romans 12:1).

12. In this lesson, a decision is a _____ , while choices mean a _____ .

B. WHAT INFLUENCE DOES SIN HAVE ON CHOICES?

Do not love the world or the things in the world. If anyone loves the world, the love of the Father is not in him. For all that is in the world—the lust of the flesh, the lust of the eyes, and the pride of life—is not of the Father but is of the world. (1 John 2:15-16)

1. The lust of the flesh is fulfilling bodily desires.

    a. This is not _____ God created in us, e.g., air, exercise, food, etc.

    b. This is _____ , e.g., illicit sex, drug addictions, alcohol, gluttony, body worship with exercise, cosmetic surgery, etc.

2. The lust of the eyes wants things we see that we don't need or shouldn't have.

    a. This is not seeing things we _____ to live, serve God, and grow to maturity.

    b. This is lusting after things to fulfill an evil desire, e.g., money, stuff, things, gadgets, or

    _____ . "Thou shalt not covet thy neighbor's house" (Exodus 20:17).

3. The pride of life is exalting self beyond what is legal or what God wants for us.

    a. Pride is not self-respect, self-confidence, or self-acceptance, which we must have for a

    _____ .

b. Pride is seeking to be something we are not and something we shouldn't be, e.g., _____ , position, _____ , glory, or exaltation.

C. PEOPLE WHO MADE BAD CHOICES

1. Lot chose the "well-watered plains" and lost _____ .

2. Samson chose "sex" and lost his _____ .

3. Achan chose covetousness: "When I saw among the spoils a beautiful Babylonian garment, two hundred shekels of silver, and a wedge of gold weighing fifty shekels, I coveted them and took them" (Joshua 7:21). Achan was _____ .

4. The rich young ruler chose _____ . "He had great possessions" (Mark 10:22)

5. Demas chose a _____ . "Demas hath forsaken me, having loved this present world" (2 Timothy 4:10, KJV).

D. PEOPLE WHO MADE GOOD CHOICES

1. Joshua. "Choose you this day whom you will serve ... but as for me and my house, we will serve the Lord" (Joshua 24:15).

   a. He had a lifetime of good choices.

   b. He was "faithful to death" (Revelation 2:10).

2. Ruth. "Thy God shall be my God" (Ruth 1:16).

   a. She chose when no one encouraged or supported her decision.

   b. She chose when there was _____ .

3. Esther. "If I perish, I perish" (Esther 4:16).

   a. She chose when there were no other options.

   b. She chose knowing she could _____ .

4. Solomon chose wisdom.

    *At Gibeon the Lord appeared to Solomon in a dream by night;
    and God said, "Ask! What shall I give you?" "Therefore, give to
    Your servant an understanding heart to judge Your people, that I
    may discern between good and evil. For who is able to judge this
    great people of Yours?" The speech pleased the Lord, that Solomon
    had asked this thing. Then God said to him: "Because you have
    asked this thing, and have not asked long life for yourself, nor have
    asked riches for yourself, nor have asked the life of your enemies,
    but have asked for yourself understanding to discern justice, And
    I have also given you what you have not asked: both riches and
    honor, so that there shall not be anyone like you among the kings
    all your days." (1 Kings 3:5,9-12)*

    a. We don't know what will happen to the things we

        _____ .

    b. The greatest choice is to be _____ .

Lesson 4:

HOW TO MAKE GOOD CHOICES FOR YOUR LIFE

A. WHAT IS A CHOICE?

1. The **freedom** of choice, e.g., do I choose steak or hot dog from the menu?

2. The **priority** of choice. You choose because inwardly you want it.

3. The **thing** chosen, e.g., I chose the early class.

4. The **variety** from which your decision is made, e.g., many kinds of chocolate.

5. Synonym: **select**, pick, elect, **prefer**, decide, **will**.

B. WHEN YOUR CHOICE
IS ALREADY MADE

1. You can't choose to worship idols. "Thou shalt have no other gods before Me" (Exodus 20:3). Don't choose to put **anything before God**. Because of enjoyment, **fear**, need, fame, **social pressure**.

2. You cannot choose to use God's name in vain. "For the Lord will not hold him guiltless" (Exodus 20:7). Because of **habit**, anger, excitement, desire, **social pressure**.

3. You can't choose to not worship **corporately** on the Lord's Day. "Keep the Sabbath day to . . . the Lord" (Deuteronomy 5:12). "Don't neglect gathering to worship" (Hebrews 10:25, ELT).

4. 4. You can't choose to kill, lie, steal, covet, or commit adultery (see Exodus 20:13-17). God has prohibited these things, so don't desire, **think about**, contemplate, or **decide** to do any of those things.

5. You must be involved with the Great Commission. "Preach the gospel to every person" (Mark 16:15). Can't choose to ignore God's initiative.

6. You must support God's work. "Bring all the tithes into the storehouse" (Malachi 3:10). Can't choose to not give.

C. WHEN YOU MAKE THE "NO" CHOICE

1. When you know and choose against God, "Don't refuse Him who speaks" (Hebrews 12:25).

    a. You harden your heart; His voice **gets fainter**.

    b. It's possible to drown out His voice **altogether**.

2. When you don't realize and choose against God. "We must give the more earnest heed . . . lest we drift away" (Hebrews 2:1).

    a. A positive yes makes the next voice more available.

    b. A positive yes makes the next decision easier.

D. CHOICES YOU DIDN'T MAKE

1. Your **parents** determine your finances.

2. Your **culture** forms your natural **values and attitudes**.

3. Your sex guided **physical** decisions.

4. Your brothers, sisters, and relatives influence you.

5. God chose you before **you chose Him**. "Chosen us in Him before the foundation of the world" (Ephesians 1:4).

6. Christ died for our sins **before we asked**. "The lamb slain before the foundation of the world" (1 Peter 1:20, ELT). "Takes away the sin of the world" (John 1:29).

E. 14 LIFE-CHANGING DECISIONS YOU MUST MAKE

1. **Salvation**. God chose **you**. "You have not chosen Me, but I have chosen you" (John 15:16). You choose **God**. "Choose you this day whom you will serve" (Joshua 24:15).

2. Whether you will be **holy and separate**. "I plead with you to give your bodies to God . . . as a living and holy sacrifice" (Romans 12:1, NLT).

3. **Marriage**. Marriage is a choice, e.g., partner, **lifestyle**, type of life, etc.

4. **Occupation**. You choose your job, but it also chooses you depending on what you can do.

5. **Education**. You choose how smart you want to be. "If you will seek wisdom ... then you will understand the right ways" (Proverbs 2:1,9, ELT).

6. **Faithfulness** to God. You choose how diligently you will follow Christ and how diligently you will work in life. "Those who seek me diligently will find me" (Proverbs 8:17).

7. Whether you will keep your **mind and body** clean. "We fight to capture every thought until it acknowledges the authority of Christ" (2 Corinthians 10:5, Phillips).

8. What kind of friends will you make?

   a. You choose friends who are like you, but

   b. You will be influenced to become like your friends, so

   c. Your choice of friends determines **your life**. "As iron sharpens iron, so a man sharpens the countenance of his friend" (Proverbs 27:17).

9. Whether you will be a **happy or angry** person. "Happy is the man that findeth wisdom" (Proverbs 3:13, KJV).

10. Whether you will be an obedient person or will **walk on the edge**. Call it **curiosity**, inquisitiveness, rebellion, or strongheadedness.

11. What kind of appearance will you make? **Neat**, appropriate, **grungy**, dirty, **immaculate**.

12. How you react to failure and success. You can't control what **happens to you**, but you can control what happens in you.

13. How you will serve the Lord. God calls and leads, but you must **follow and act**.

14. Where you will **live**. Choices made by **occupation**, income, **self-perception**, mate, God's leading, etc.

Lesson 4:

QUESTIONS

HOW TO MAKE GOOD CHOICES FOR YOUR LIFE

A. WHAT IS A CHOICE?

1. The _____ of choice, e.g., do I choose steak or hot dog from the menu?

2. The _____ of choice. You choose because inwardly you want it.

3. The _____ chosen, e.g., I chose the early class.

4. The _____ from which your decision is made, e.g., many kinds of chocolate.

5. Synonym: _____ , pick, elect, _____ , decide, _____ .

B. WHEN YOUR CHOICE
IS ALREADY MADE

1. You can't choose to worship idols. "Thou shalt have no other gods before Me" (Exodus 20:3). Don't choose to put _____ . Because of enjoyment, **fear**, need, fame, _____ .

2. You cannot choose to use God's name in vain. "For the Lord will not hold him guiltless" (Exodus 20:7). Because of _ _____ , anger, excitement, desire, _____ .

3. You can't choose to not worship _____ on the Lord's Day. "Keep the Sabbath day to . . . the Lord" (Deuteronomy 5:12). "Don't neglect gathering to worship" (Hebrews 10:25, ELT).

4. 4. You can't choose to kill, lie, steal, covet, or commit adultery (see Exodus 20:13-17). God has prohibited these things, so don't des ire, _____ , contemplate, or _____ to do any of those things.

5. You must be involved with the Great Commission. "Preach the gospel to every person" (Mark 16:15). Can't choose to ignore God's initiative.

6. You must support God's work. "Bring all the tithes into the storehouse" (Malachi 3:10). Can't choose to not give.

C. WHEN YOU MAKE THE "NO" CHOICE

1. When you know and choose against God, "Don't refuse Him who speaks" (Hebrews 12:25).

    a. You harden your heart; His voice _____ .

    b. It's possible to drown out His voice _____ .

2. When you don't realize and choose against God. "We must give the more earnest heed . . . lest we drift away" (Hebrews 2:1).

    a. A positive yes makes the next voice more available.

    b. A positive yes makes the next decision easier.

D. CHOICES YOU DIDN'T MAKE

1. Your _____ determine your finances.

2. Your _____ forms your natural
   _____ .

3. Your sex guided _____ decisions.

4. Your brothers, sisters, and relatives influence you.

5. God chose you before _____ .
   "Chosen us in Him before the foundation of the world"
   (Ephesians 1:4).

6. Christ died for our sins _____ .
   "The lamb slain before the foundation of the world"
   (1 Peter 1:20, ELT). "Takes away the sin of the world" (John 1:29).

E. 14 LIFE-CHANGING DECISIONS YOU MUST MAKE

1. _____ . God chose _____ . "You have
   not chosen Me, but I have chosen you" (John 15:16). You choose
   _____ . "Choose you this day whom you will serve"
   (Joshua 24:15).

2. Whether you will be _____ . "I
   plead with you to give your bodies to God . . . as a living and holy
   sacrifice" (Romans 12:1, NLT).

3. _____ . Marriage is a choice, e.g., partner,
   _____ , type of life, etc.

4. _____ . You choose your job, but it also chooses you
   depending on what you can do.

5. _____ . You choose how smart you want to be. "If
   you will seek wisdom ... then you will understand the right ways"
   (Proverbs 2:1,9, ELT).

6. _____ to God. You choose how diligently you will
   follow Christ and how diligently you will work in life. "Those who
   seek me diligently will find me" (Proverbs 8:17).

7. Whether you will keep your _____
   clean. "We fight to capture every thought until it acknowledges the
   authority of Christ" (2 Corinthians 10:5, Phillips).

8. What kind of friends will you make?

   a. You choose friends who are like you, but

   b. You will be influenced to become like your friends, so

   c. Your choice of friends determines _____. "As
      iron sharpens iron, so a man sharpens the countenance of his
      friend" (Proverbs 27:17).

9. Whether you will be a _____
   person. "Happy is the man that findeth wisdom"
   (Proverbs 3:13, KJV).

10. Whether you will be an obedient person or will
    _____. Call it **curiosity**,
    inquisitiveness, rebellion, or strongheadedness.

11. What kind of appearance will you make? _____ ,
    appropriate, _____ , dirty, _____ .

12. How you react to failure and success. You can't control what
    _____ , but you can control
    what happens in you.

13. How you will serve the Lord. God calls and leads, but you must

    _____ .

14. Where you will _____ . Choices made by
    _____ , income, _____ , mate, God's
    leading, etc.

MAKING CHOICES WITH GOD'S HELP

A. INTRODUCTION

1. Begin by realizing God has a **plan/purpose** for your life. "I have a plan for your life for good and not evil" (Jeremiah 29:11, ELT).

2. Then realize God has **right choices** for you. "Let God transform you into a new person by changing the way you think. Then you will know what God wants you to do and how ... perfect His will really is" (Romans 12:2, NLT).

3. God is concerned about every **big and little** choice.

   a. Big choices determine your **destiny**.

   b. Many little choices make up **big things** that reflect your **character**.

   c. There are no little choices in eternity.

4. Live a yielded life so God is your **primary concern**.

5. But still, many don't know **what to do**. "What to choose, I know not" (Philippians 1:22, ELT).

B. HELPS TO FIND AND MAKE GOD'S CHOICES

Who are those who fear the Lord, He will show them the path they should choose. (Psalm 25:12, NLT)

1. Good choices are **consistent** with the Word of God.

    a. Don't make choices contrary to what you know is **right**. "To choose what is right and reject what is wrong" (Isaiah 7:16, NLT).

    b. Follow **positive** principles, i.e., obey, pray, etc.

    c. The Bible may not tell you what to do but it will give you a **context** to make choices.

    d. Gives you **guidelines** for living. "I am determined to obey you until I die" (Psalm 119:112, TLB).

2. Prayer **guides** you into right choices.

    a. Pray early **each** day about all choices. "Seek first the kingdom of God" (Matthew 6:33).

    b. Pray constantly about **big** choices, e.g., mate, job, etc.

    c. In prayer you are **slowly conformed** into God's likeness.

    d. To wait and pray gives God a chance to work. "We can make our plans, but the Lord determines our steps" (Proverbs 16:9, NLT).

3. Make all choices in view of God's work for your life. "Not my will but thine be done" (Matthew 26:34).

    a. If you **fight God**, what you don't want to do may be His will.

    b. b. If you are **yielded to God**, what you want to do may be His will.

4. Make choices in view of your **strengths** or spiritual giftedness.

    a. God doesn't want everyone in **full-time** service.

    b. God wants everyone **full time** wherever they work. "Everyone has his own particular gift from God" (1 Corinthians 7:7, Phillips).

5. Listen to counsel from **mature family and friends** when making choices. "Plans go wrong for lack of advice" (Proverbs 15:22, NLT). "In the multitude of counselors, there is safety" (Proverbs 11:14).

    a. Ask, "What would Jesus do?" (WWJD)

    b. You see the issues **objectively** when you explain to another.

    c. Your counselor makes you think of **consequences** and the other side.

6. The right choice may be found by common sense. Definition: **practical** shrewdness, normal intelligence, **Grandpa's advice**.

    a. Only seldom does God lead **contrary** to common sense.

    b. Check your decision with Scripture.

7. The right choice can be found through **circumstances**.

    a. Take **opportunities** of open doors. "There is a wide-open door for a great work here" (1 Corinthians 16:9, NLT).

    b. **Closed doors** can be wonderful.

    c. Accept **positive assurance** from bad choices.

8. God shows His will to those who are actively serving Him. Illustration: **sailboat**.

C. WHAT IS GOD'S WILL FOR YOUR LIFE?

1. A blueprint.

    a. All choices are made for you.

    b. If you make wrong choices, you have God's **permissive** will.

    c. Very few find the **center** but spend their life on the periphery.

2. A **compass**.

    a. Guides you from your present **location**.

    b. Always points to right choices, no matter how many times you **get lost**.

    c. Never assumes you are in the **wrong place**.

Lesson 5:

QUESTIONS

MAKING CHOICES WITH GOD'S HELP

A. INTRODUCTION

1. Begin by realizing God has a _____ for your life. "I have a plan for your life for good and not evil" (Jeremiah 29:11, ELT).

2. Then realize God has _____ for you. "Let God transform you into a new person by changing the way you think. Then you will know what God wants you to do and how ... perfect His will really is" (Romans 12:2, NLT).

3. God is concerned about every _____ choice.

   a. Big choices determine your _____ .

   b. Many little choices make up _____ that reflect your _____ .

   c. There are no little choices in eternity.

4. Live a yielded life so God is your _____ .

5. But still, many don't know _____ .
   "What to choose, I know not" (Philippians 1:22, ELT).

B. HELPS TO FIND AND MAKE GOD'S CHOICES

Who are those who fear the Lord, He will show them the path they should choose. (Psalm 25:12, NLT)

1. Good choices are _____ with the Word of God.

    a. Don't make choices contrary to what you know is _____ . "To choose what is right and reject what is wrong" (Isaiah 7:16, NLT).

    b. Follow _____ principles, i.e., obey, pray, etc.

    c. The Bible may not tell you what to do but it will give you a _____ to make choices.

    d. Gives you _____ for living. "I am determined to obey you until I die" (Psalm 119:112, TLB).

2. Prayer _____ you into right choices.

    a. Pray early _____ day about all choices. "Seek first the kingdom of God" (Matthew 6:33).

    b. Pray constantly about _____ choices, e.g., mate, job, etc.

    c. In prayer you are _____ into God's likeness.

    d. To wait and pray gives God a chance to work. "We can make our plans, but the Lord determines our steps" (Proverbs 16:9, NLT).

3. Make all choices in view of God's work for your life. "Not my will but thine be done" (Matthew 26:34).

    a. If you _____ , what you don't want to do may be His will.

    b. b. If you are _____ , what you want to do may be His will.

4. Make choices in view of your _____ or spiritual giftedness.

    a. God doesn't want everyone in _____ service.

    b. God wants everyone _____ wherever they work. "Everyone has his own particular gift from God" (1 Corinthians 7:7, Phillips).

5. Listen to counsel from _____ when making choices. "Plans go wrong for lack of advice" (Proverbs 15:22, NLT). "In the multitude of counselors, there is safety" (Proverbs 11:14).

    a. Ask, "What would Jesus do?" (WWJD)

    b. You see the issues _____ when you explain to another.

    c. Your counselor makes you think of _____ and the other side.

The right choice may be found by common sense. Definition: _____ shrewdness, normal intelligence, _____ .

    a. Only seldom does God lead _____ to common sense.

    b. Check your decision with Scripture.

6. The right choice can be found through _____ .

   a. Take _____ of open doors. "There is a wide-open door for a great work here" (1 Corinthians 16:9, NLT).

   b. _____ can be wonderful.

   c. Accept _____ from bad choices.

7. God shows His will to those who are actively serving Him. Illustration: _____ .

C. WHAT IS GOD'S WILL FOR YOUR LIFE?

1. A blueprint.

   a. All choices are made for you.

   b. If you make wrong choices, you have God's _____ will.

   c. Very few find the _____ but spend their life on the periphery.

2. A _____ .

   a. Guides you from your present _____ .

   b. Always points to right choices, no matter how many times you _____ .

   c. Never assumes you are in the _____ .

PART FOUR

FAITH
WALKING
through
PROBLEMS

ADDITIONAL RESOURCES

POWERPOINT SLIDES:

To purchase and download the Powerpoint Slides go to
https://www.norimediagroup.com/pages/elmer-towns

VIDEO:

To purchase available video by Dr. Towns go to
https://www.norimediagroup.com/pages/elmer-towns

ADD-ON CONTENT

To purchase additional products in this series go to
https://www.norimediagroup.com/pages/elmer-towns

RELATED BOOKS

My Name is the Holy Spirit: Discover Me through My Name
Available at https://www.norimediagroup.com/pages/elmer-towns

From

ELMER L. TOWNS

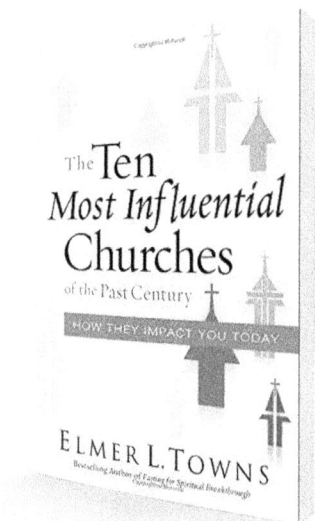

Your Church Can Influence the World

History has shown that great leaders have the ability to reach beyond the walls of their churches to influence cultures for Christ. We've seen it in the Pentecostal/Charismatic movement, in the explosive growth of house churches in Communist China, in the expansion of the Southern Baptist Convention, and in the worldwide rise of praise and worship music led by Hillsong Church, among other phenomena.

In *The Ten Most Influential Churches of the Past Century*, Dr. Elmer Towns presents evidence of the powerful influence of these churches and how their innovative strategies and faith accomplish these goals. Then he tells how you can apply these principles to your church. You will learn how some of the most influential leaders in Church history became conduits for your future ministry and how your church can experience exponential growth.

Most importantly, you will see that the great results in these ten churches grow out of the power of the Word of God, the ministry of many dedicated lay workers, the faith-producing ministry of great leaders—all under the anointing of the Holy Spirit.

Purchase your copy wherever books are sold

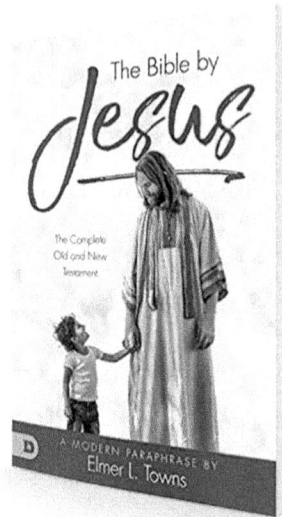

From

ELMER L. TOWNS

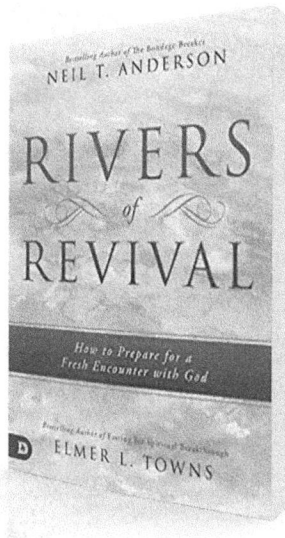

Since the Day of Pentecost, seasons of revival and awakening have brought refreshing to the spiritually dry, life to the spiritually dead, and miraculous encounters with the Holy Spirit.

In this timely and prophetic volume, two bestselling generals of the faith, Dr. Elmer Towns and Dr. Neil T. Anderson, offer collective wisdom, insight, and strategy on how you can experience and release a river of Holy Spirit outpouring into your world!

Additionally, Drs. Towns and Anderson have compiled contributions from other key authorities on revival who have encountered the move of God firsthand. Each contributor provides practical wisdom on how you can experience the Spirit's touch in your own life, church and even geographical region.

A fresh move of God is on the way. Prepare yourself to experience Holy Spirit outpouring like never before!

Purchase your copy wherever books are sold

From
ELMER L. TOWNS

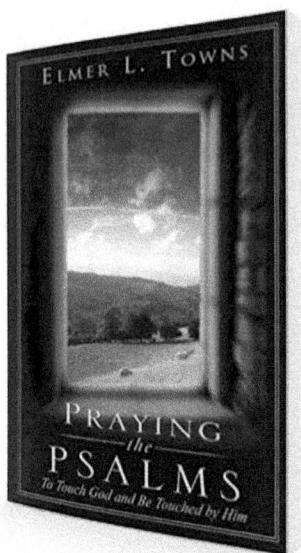

The Book of Psalms reflects the heart of God. *Praying the Psalms* carefully shapes the Psalms into personal prayers enabling you to identify with the Psalmist as he prayed. The author, Dr. Towns, is living breathing testimony of the power and fulfillment you will experience as you read the pages of this most powerful book.

The Psalmist poured our his soul to God concerning the things that deeply moved him. As you read the Psalms, you are taking a peak into his heart. You will weep when he weeps, should when he rejoices, burn when he gets angry and fall on your face when he worships God.

Purchase your copy wherever books are sold